LIFE AT HOME;

OR,

THE FAMILY AND ITS MEMBERS.

BY

WILLIAM AIKMAN, D.D.

The pilgrim's step in vain
  Seeks Eden's sacred ground!
But in Home's holy joys again,
  An Eden may be found.

BOWRING.

NEW YORK:
SAMUEL R. WELLS, PUBLISHER,
NO. 389 BROADWAY.
1870.

E. O. JENKINS,
STEREOTYPER AND PRINTER,
20 N. WILLIAM ST., N. Y.

TO

My Wife,

WHOSE LIFE HAS GIVEN THE IDEAL OF THE PLEASANT

PICTURES I HAVE TRIED TO DRAW,

IN THE

FOLLOWING PAGES,

OF

DAUGHTER AND SISTER, WIFE AND MOTHER,

This Book

IS

DEDICATED.

PREFACE.

THE following pages substantially were preached as a series of discourses to the people of the writer's pastoral charge. The favor with which they were received and the request of the publisher have led him to believe that their issue in a more permanent form might be desirable and useful.

At a time when the sacredness of the marriage relation is so much called in question, and when the bonds which hold the family together are in danger of being lightly esteemed, any attempt to exalt the family life may be hopeful of good.

The failure to reach the highest happiness of married life, and the best results of family training are caused, we may believe, not so much by willfulness as by ignorance or inexperience. If, at the outset, a few cautions and suggestions, founded on maturer thought and larger observation, were received, mistakes could be corrected and errors avoided which too often occasion long years of disappointment and sorrow. If this book shall make such suggestions, its design will be accomplished.

The Bible is incomparably the best manual for the regulation of the family. In these chapters much has been made of its teachings, and it will be an unspeakable reward if the writer shall have done anything to enhance its value in any home.

All that is hopeful for our country and the world is from the family. Christian homes are the want of the world. Have them, and the future of the Church and therefore the well-being of the race is secure. These pages are sent forth with a very deep desire to bring, if possible, the blessed light of the Gospel of the Lord Jesus Christ into the family circle. That light will fill any home with a radiance of peace and joy.

NEW YORK, March 24, 1870.

CONTENTS.

I.

THE FAMILY RELATION.

The family an arrangement of God — The narrative of the Creation — Convents, associations, phalanxes, contrary to divine appointments — The family necessary for the development of the race — Christianity gives the highest ideal of the family — The Bible descriptions of the family — Polygamy: the Bible argument against it — The family for the preservation of the race — The family for the development of character — Transformations — The family multiplies human happiness — The family the refuge place — The family the educator of the race — Citizens made by the family — The family must have a home — Family boarding — Its evils — Nuptial crime — Children gifts of God — The beauty and blessedness of a family — The family changes. *Page* 13

II.

HUSBANDS AND WIVES.

The Lord's announcement — The sacredness and purity of the marriage relation — Celibacy against nature — Paul's assertions — Nature and the Providence of God regulates — A man's or a woman's character properly developed only in the married state — Old maids and old bachelors — Marriage an entrance on a new world — Unity of feeling to be cultivated — No secrets between husband and wife — Gossip — Understanding one another — Forbearance with each other

— Changes seen after marriage — New discoveries — The beginnings of estrangements — Demonstrations of affection to be given — The Bible to be read together — Prayer with each other. *Page* 36

III.

HUSBANDS.

Christ's love for the Church — Presumption in the offer of marriage — The completeness of a wife's surrender of herself — The greatness of the assumed charge — The old home and loves abandoned — The wife's claim on all of her husband's heart — The surrender of the husband as absolute as the wife's surrender — Sympathy demanded — The wife's exhaustive cares — Unreasonable requirements — Selfishness and thoughtlessness — Consultation with a wife — A woman's intuition — Affection to be shown — Demonstration of love not to be confined to the days of courtship — The power of little attentions — The lover a husband — Politeness to a wife — A wife longs for expressions of love — The fire of love never to go out — Husbands of Christian wives — The prayers of a Christian wife. *Page* 65

IV.

WIVES.

"I did not promise to obey" — The old words of the Bible not obsolete — Obedience in the heart of the wife — Reverence the beginning of love — Love sees much — The husband the head of the household — Women do not admire the master-women — Authority felt, love gone — The true wife glories in her reverence for her husband — The husband before all others — Intimate friends to be left outside — Grievances to be hidden in the wife's bosom — A husband's love to be kept — Same care to keep as to win love — Love should grow deeper as years grow on — The delicacy of early days — Personal attractiveness — Cultivation of the mind — Physical attractiveness — The "market made" — Home to be made pleasant — Sunshine of looks and words — Contentment and satisfaction — Little and delicate attentions to be shown — Care of a husband's interests — Defence of a husband to the last — Pious wives and irreligious husbands — The power of a good wife. *Page* 89

V.

PARENTS.

Parental responsibility not realized—The signet—The two pictures —Parental power to shape the soul—The Abrahamic commendation—The future of a child's life can be predicted—God's guidance—Right appreciation of parental influence—Sympathy with childhood—The by-gone days of childhood to be kept in mind—Children's love to be kept—Confiding in a parent—Home to be made attractive—The meals joyous—Games and pastimes—Birthdays and holidays to be kept—The heart to be cultivated as well as the head—Demonstrations of affection not to be slighted—Obedience to be secured so as to win love—Children to be trained for usefulness and independence—Politeness in the family—Christianity makes gentlemen—Prayer for help—Consecration to God for children. *Page* 118

VI.

CHILDREN.

The place in the Decalogue of the Fifth Commandment—Its promise fulfilled—Children under the parental roof—A parent's love—Its devotion—Respect and honor to be shown—Confidence in parents—Consultations with them about companions and reading—Immoral Books—Beauty of familiar intercourse between parents and children—Filial devotion—Story from Heroditus—The daughter and son show what the wife and husband will be—Visiting parents—Writing to parents—Filial neglect—Heart sorrows caused by negligence and thoughtlessness—Care of aged parents—The wooden trough—Regrets over the dead. *Page* 151

VII.

BROTHERS AND SISTERS.

The family a delicate mechanism—Brothers and sisters must be in adjustment—Boys and girls not the same—The boy baby—The girl baby—Tom-boys—Character developed by differences of disposition—Holding affection—Sympathy with each other—Confidence and intimacy to be cultivated—A sister's love—The childhood days—Pictures painted for the by and by—Polite attentions between brothers and sisters — The good sisters and brothers make the good wives and husbands — Sisters should protect their brothers — Brothers should guard the reputation of their sisters — The immoral to be cast out from the presence of a pure girl — Girls do not know their power — Brothers to stand together — The old man and the rods — Brothers helping brothers — Family quarrels — The old love to be called up — Associations and intimacies to be kept up between brothers. *Page* 177

VIII.

EMPLOYERS AND EMPLOYED.

Two classes always in the world, employers and employed — They cannot be separated — They depend on each other — Mental characteristics make employment necessary for some — Labor honorable — Allotments of life made by God — The employed to give all his time and skill — Waste — Antagonisms between capital and labor — Demagogues — Capital the friend and support of labor — Aspirations for higher places — Fill well the lower places — Employers should identify themselves with the employed — Pay what is honest and fair — Pay promptly and regularly — Cruelty — Interest in the moral character of the employed — Interest in the future of the employed — The mistress — Sympathy with her servants — Inspire respect — Speak encouraging words—Patience and kindness — Be Christian with your servants. *Page* 198

IX.

THE ALTAR IN THE HOUSE.

Religion twofold, heart and life—Demands "an outward manifestation" — The temple grows out of the closet — Family religion — It must have an outward form — Family worship a necessity of the family life — Reflex power of the family altar on the parent — The family altar a help to family training — The being and presence of God made real by the family altar — God's word divine there — The power of family prayer — Thoughts and resolutions of a child — Excuses for the neglect of family worship — Children often wonder at the neglect — Remorse — An incident — Rules and suggestions for family worship — Form and manner of observance — The infant's prayer — Scenes of the future — The by-gone days — Memories. *Page* 226

CHAPTER I.

THE FAMILY RELATION.

God setteth the solitary in families.—PSALM lxviii. 6.

O bliss of blissful hours!
The boon of Heaven's decreeing,
While yet in Eden's bowers
Dwelt the First Husband and his sinless mate!
The one sweet plant which, piteous Heaven agreeing,
They bore with them through Eden's closing gate,
COLERIDGE.

THE Family is not an accident, but rather the all-wise arrangement of the Great Creator, by which the well-being of man is to be promoted. All the divine appointments are such as have a tendency to lift man to the highest possible point as an intellectual and moral being, and the Family Relation, perhaps above all others, is intended to produce this result.

It is greatly worthy of our thought why the

fact of man's solitariness and need of a companion, as well as the closeness of the union subsisting between husband and wife, should have been so carefully and so strikingly exhibited in the narrative of the creation. The exigencies of man's nature, at least, are here recognized — It is not good that man should be alone. Perhaps also it was for the very purpose that men should in every age of the world be taught to set the highest possible value on the family, and to be alert to gather the wide harvest of blessedness which it produces.

The anchorite in his cell is a man not only at war with his own nature, but he is offending against the highest good of human society. So, too, all the schemes which men have invented to take the place of the family, by a substitution of associations, leagues, phalanxes, always have been unsuccessful. They have contained the elements of their own dissolution, because they have sought to abrogate the first great appointment of God. The family was constituted by Him, and nothing of human device can take its place or do its work. Men have tried again and again, they have banded themselves together, and in a thousand ways sought to reach what they vainly deemed better results, but whether they were the monasteries of St. Anthony, or the associations of Fourier, their inventions have wrought out the same bad product, and have shown that God knew and that the Bible teaches what is best for man.

The Family is necessary for the development of the race. There can be no true development without it. The savage state knows little of the family. In the lowest types of humanity, such as the Bushmen of South Africa, it is almost unknown. Children are born, but as soon as they are able to care for their own wants, they wander off and are lost among the rest of the tribe, as a lamb is merged in the surrounding flock, and all connection between parents and their offspring is quickly lost. In tribes more elevated, but still barbaric—our American Indians may be an example—the same fact is seen; the family, such as it is in its true idea, is scarcely to be recognized. Husbands and wives may live in the same hut, and children may remain for a while near it, but all that intercourse and association which make the family is unknown. There is natural affection, often pure and deep, between individuals, but no general bond of sympathy and love holding the whole group together as a unity.

Civilization varies with the family and the family with civilization. Its highest and most complete realization is found where the enlightenment of Christianity prevails, where woman is exalted to her true and lofty place as equal with the man, where husband and wife are one in honor, in influence, in affection, and where children are a common bond of care and love. Here you have the idea of a perfect family.

Here is one of those innumerable, but powerful, because indirect and unannounced, proofs of the supernatural character of the Bible. What book of ancient times gives such pictures of the family life—what book such precepts for family government? How wonderful it is, that these old books, written many of them in those far back centuries which antedate historic records, do give us such advanced ideas! Here is a book which in this regard was clearly made not for that time alone, but for all time, not for society as it then was, but for society in its highest state—for civilization in its very best form. Paint for yourself your brightest conception of what a family should be, have husband and wife living in pure and blissful companionship; father and mother wise and loving, yet sovereign; surround the fireside with perfect children, children who are just what you would have them, affectionate, obedient, joyous; let brothers and sisters be linked together in unwavering and kindly sympathy, in love as strong and glowing as your imagination can picture; then look into the Bible. You shall find that very family set before you, you shall see all the exhortations and injunctions of this Book looking toward just such a home.

Proof from the Bible is sometimes asked against the practice of polygamy. I reply that the whole Bible is against it, from the first chapter, where God said, "I will make a helpmeet for him," to the last, where the "Bride the Lamb's wife" is seen descending out of heaven from God. And every metaphor, without, as far as I know, an exception, has in view simply and only one wife. To add a plural would be to rob figure and illustration of all their force and beauty, and in many cases to make them only absurd.

The first creation was that of one wife. Why, when the earth was to be peopled, when, if ever, it would be expedient and necessary that there should be a plurality of wives, why were not more than one created, if the well-being of man were best promoted by such an arrangement?

And what was the fact at the beginning, has been continued as a fact ever since. The race has been propagated in pairs, with a continuance and precision which is wholly inexplicable on any other theory than that of an original intention of the Creator and Preserver of men. An equal number of each sex has been born into the world from century to century, through all the variations of time and circumstances, and has perpetually been declaring that one husband with one wife meets and fills the idea of the nuptial relation.

Our Lord's words, "They twain shall be one flesh"—A man shall leave father and mother, and "shall cleave to his wife," point unerringly to the same truth, and clearly do not countenance, even by implication, a plurality. A man shall cleave to his three wives! They four shall be one flesh! You smile at the absurdity, while the grand and beautiful truth which He taught has vanished away.

This general drift of the Bible, an equatorial

current that sweeps in one direction through it all, is to my mind a mightier argument than a direct precept could have been. An announced command might be limited and confined to the time and the circumstances in which it was given, and its force be evaded, as many ordinances of the Bible are, by arguments built upon the changes of the ages. Not so this, which through all the forty centuries of the Bible, presents the same conception of the family life, upon which every figure and illustration is based.

That ideal of the family contemplates and can contemplate only one husband and one wife. It presents one father and one mother at its head, and children who are fruit and pledge of their one love. Think, if you can without a smile, of a family gathering round the family altar, where the father, as priest of the house, offers up their worship, with a number of wives and mothers around him, his wives and their mothers! Is it a very congruous or beautiful picture? Is it a lovely type of the church of Christ or of the family in heaven?

No, polygamy is born not out of the chastity but out of the lusts of men. Only what is animal in man asks for it. No true man desires more than one wife, and that wife ceases to be a woman in the highest and holiest sense when another woman sits equal with her as wife and mother. All that is purest and best in us cries out, Let there be one husband round whom one wife can throw her arms and say, proudly and joyfully, "He is mine, mine alone! I know that no other is on the throne of his heart!" Let there be one wife upon whom a husband may look, while he holds her to his bosom with inexpressible affection and says, "She is beyond and above all others dearer and better. I want none else, she is queen of my heart and life!"

A relation so clearly ordained, cannot but be intended by the Creator to subserve important purposes for humanity. At the very outset we can see that the family is intended for the preservation of the race. Looking at man merely as an animal, how perfectly the family meets his necessities. It has been often remarked, and every one has thought it, as he has looked upon the poor feeble form of a young infant, its little thin fingers grasping at vacancy, its head supported on the nurse's hand, that of all living things born into this world a human being is the most absolutely helpless. It is as if the greatness of its destiny were to be measured by the abjectness of its beginning. But this helpless thing is welcomed by those whose hearts bound with an unknown thrill at its first cry—

> "There are smiles and tears in the mother's eyes,
> For her new-born babe beside her lies;
> Oh heaven of bliss! when the heart o'erflows
> With the rapture a mother only knows."

Who of you, that are parents, will ever forget that feeble wail of your first-born? You had heard the voice of infancy before; it had awakened feelings perhaps of petulancy and annoyance; but why, now, is that sound like nothing that you ever heard before, and why does it touch a chord whose vibrations tremble through all your nature? Ah! it is the voice of *your* child! No other voice hath ever had such a tone as that!

And this is but a type of all that follows in the child's life. It comes into the family where henceforth it is to be guarded and preserved. Its life becomes a solicitude and a care, its health becomes a means of family happiness, and all the great interests of father and mother are made to depend on its well being. Its sickness throws a pall of foreboding over the household, its death a sorrow that is never removed. What a perpetual inducement, then, the family creates for the preservation of the race!

The family is the great means for the development of character. What a world does it present for the affections to abide in! Where on all the earth beside are sympathies so warm, love so pure and fervent as here? All that gives value or beauty to human character finds in the family at once an atmosphere in which to expand and develop the elements which shall bring it to the highest perfection.

The family creates a perpetual power which holds and moves evermore each individual of the circle. The parental love, evoked every hour in providing, watching, guiding, throws back its influence over the heart and life of father and mother, and makes them what they never could be without it; it is a power which tends all the time to lift them to a higher and better place.

Who has not seen with half wonder the sudden development of a young couple when once they have become father and mother? A few days ago—yesterday it seems—and they were almost children; the young wife was a girl with all the joyous carelessness and heedless buoyancy of a child; her older friends, at least those who had not thought enough, shook their heads dubiously and told one another that she was "fit for anything but to be married;" "she might better be at home with her mother, or even at her school." But the wife becomes a mother, and a marvellous transformation comes to pass. There may be the same vivacity and spirit, but all is calmer, deeper, stronger. She has entered a new world, and is endued with new powers. A wise providence has taken the place of thoughtlessness, a firm self-reliance that of helpless dependence, an untiring energy that of dreamy inactivity. The girl has suddenly become a woman, challenging your respect with your admiration.

Nor is this unseen but all-potent force diminished as the years advance. In this charmed atmosphere of the family all the capabilities of the parents' nature are brought out and enlarged; characteristics of grace and beauty spring into life, which elsewhere would have lain dormant and unknown. Here are influences which reach out as with angel hands and sweep over the soul, waking into melody chords which no other touch could move. A father or a mother walks in a world all unknown to those who have never had a child, a world of thought and experiences and powers which lies quite beyond their ken; and the parent whose character is not developed into rounder form and fairer symmetry because he is a parent, shows that there is something wanting in his own nature.

The family is God's appointed means of multiplying human happiness. When man fell he lost his hold on eternal and temporal bliss. Eden had in it enough to satisfy all his natural and physical cravings, and with the lovely and beloved wife whom God had given him, there was sympathy and sweet society sufficient to make full his cup of earthly happiness. With his fall he lost paradise, and went out a driven and homeless wanderer in a world which was henceforth to be an unfriendly world. But the tender compassion of God taking much away from him, spared him what could make bearable the loss of Eden. The partner of his sin went out with him to be the partner of his sorrow and its solace. The only thing given him there which he could retain was his wife, and she was a part of Paradise. Beautifully has Cowper caught the thought:

> "Domestic happiness, their only bliss
> Of Paradise that has survived the fall.

In the "bosom of the family"—a familiar but touching expression—a man finds what earth nowhere else can give. The brotherhood of man is almost an empty name. Sin has broken it up and left it well nigh an ideal thing. Selfishness, rather, and consequent distance and coldness have become the type of human intercourse. I would not deny the actuality of friendship which has no origin in blood relationship. There is, and some of us have known it in our life, a friendship which is hallowed, which rises above the vicissitudes of time and place and circumstances; "there is a friend who sticketh closer than a brother;" but this is rare, and it is our fortune to meet such a friend only once or twice in all our life. For the most part this world is full rather of suspicion, doubt and disappointment. One who lives many years, and indeed they need not be many, will have his heart ache over bitter disappointments which he has met in his reliance on friendships which are merely earthly.

But there is a place where he comes, sick, it may be, and sad of heart, and where he knows that he shall not be disappointed. Careworn and weary he enters his home after a day of bitterness; contact with men has made all seem like Sahara's waste to him, but now a welcome greets him which has in it the aroma of heaven. Here is one who does not misunderstand; here is one who will sympathize; here are more than one who will think well of him and nothing but well; here are eyes which will look lovingly, and voices which will speak tenderly; here are hands that will smooth his aching head, a bosom on which it may lean; here are little ones that will clamber on his knee and tell him that of all in this world he is the dearest and wisest and best.

Many and many a man would not be brave enough to meet life's trials and life's labor, but would faint rather and die, would perhaps rush out of life in very despair, were it not that from the family come the calls of wife and children, like the music of angels, or a warrior's clarion, giving to him a new inspiration of energy and hope. Oh! how many a cloud of care is caught up and wafted out of sight by the gentle winds which breathe from that sacred place; how many a broad and steady gleam of sunshine gilds the pathway and lights up the head of weary toilers when their steps cross the threshold of home! This is but a type of all the rest. That strange, frightened feeling of abandonment which a lost child has, the thrill of agony so peculiar that once felt is remembered forever, is the symbol of what would be for brothers and sisters were there no home and no family life. Of all words, orphan has the deepest wail of sadness in it, since it speaks of family life and love gone out in death; and no one knows the all-pervading blessedness of the family until with choked voice he murmurs, I have no home!

The Family is the educator of the race. Here men and women are made. What they are in the world, that they were in the family as children. The family is the place where the first lessons of law are received, and where the whole character in view of law has a direction given it. The citizen is made in the family long before the time of voting or activity has come. When Napoleon said, in answer to Madame De Stael's question about France's greatest need, "Mothers," he asserted the all-potent influence of a true family life. The grand, crying want of our own land to-day is right family influence. For the lack of it the land mourns. Had families been all or even a part of what they ought to have been, perhaps most of the evils which afflicted us and imperiled our existence in the late Rebellion would not have had a being, and the lawlessness and crime which stalk abroad point back to childhood and to unblest homes.

The atmosphere of the family is what determines the constitution of the man. Each member of the family is an element of that atmosphere; father and mother and brother and sister compound it for weal or woe. In this country, while we do not undervalue the power of the family, we are in constant danger of losing its untold benefits. Our American restlessness which drives us from home over our broad country, our changes which blot out of existence the old homestead, the rush which excites and the hurry which hardens us, so that we have no time to attend to the gentler amenities of life, all admonish us to guard with special care our family influences.

Among our numerous and curious inventions, we have of late brought into popularity what is perhaps the least beautiful of them all—family boarding. To avoid expense and be rid of trouble, housekeeping is broken up, and father and mother and children make their abode in the hotel. Now I would not for a moment intimate that the boarding-house is not as necessary as it is a useful institution. Far from it. I intend to assert that it cannot make a family home; it was never intended so to do. Indeed, I might add, the experience of unhappy hosts and of guests, who have a right to be in a boarding-house, because they have no family and can have no home, mournfully testifies that however the attempt may be made to constitute it a home, the results are not lovely. As a general thing, a boarding family is a boarding nuisance.

The family must have a home, and the hotel or the boarding-house can never give it. To have a home which is not all a name, you must have a door which shall open to yours as to no other hand, a threshold upon which you step as the drawbridge to your castle, a house over which you may go with the unthought consciousness that it is yours alone. Its halls must not be the thoroughfare of a hundred passers, and your rooms your only domain.

This hotel life has a disastrous effect on a family of children. It renders family training and true government very difficult and almost impossible. If, to avoid the subtile and unfortunate results of promiscuous intercourse, the little ones are confined in their apartments, their physical as well as mental health must suffer; if they are permitted to be abroad, they are subject to influences entirely beyond parental control. If the child be interesting or sprightly, he is petted and spoiled; if he be dull or peculiar, he is soured and injured by neglect; and in either case the little one bears the unfortunate consequences of the evil circumstances by which he is inevitably surrounded.

If parents do not need a home, their children do; and though it should be the smallest of all homes, they should have one. The number of its apartments and the style of its furniture are but of small account in comparison with the thing itself. If I were advising a young married couple,

I would say: *As soon as possible make yourselves a home;* feel that married life is all incomplete without that. If you cannot get it at once, fix it as something to be striven after unfalteringly till it is obtained. It is easier to enter upon the cares and the work of house- (better say home-) keeping at once, than when the indolent habits of boarding have taken away your heart for it. While you are alone, only husband and wife, it would be better if you had a home, and tenfold more so if God should give you children.

That word, children, suggests a topic which calls for plain and emphatic words. Within the last few years a feeling has grown up the opposite of that natural sentiment of the olden time which regarded children as gifts to be desired from God. By many the man is not now accounted "happy that hath his quiver full of them." Rather they are looked upon as evils to be endured, burdens and cares which largely spoil life's enjoyments.

To be a mother, is by very many esteemed not a great privilege, a boon to be asked for, but rather a calamity to be dreaded, a doom by all means, lawful and unlawful, to be avoided. There are thousands of homes which are willfully and willingly unblest of children; and many and many a young wife lives with shattered health undermined by her own act, and many have sunk and many others are going down to premature graves because they seek to avoid what the Creator has made for every right-minded woman the highest honor and chiefest good—children who shall rise up and call her blessed. It is a growing vice and a crying shame. It is as if that Psalm, one of the "Songs of degrees," had become obsolete and false. Read it as it rang out from grateful lips in the olden time, as families went up singing on their way to Jerusalem: "Except the Lord build the house, they labor in vain that build it; except the Lord keep the city, the watchman waketh in vain. . . . . Lo, children are an heritage of the Lord; and the fruit of the womb His reward. As arrows in the hand of a mighty man, so are children of the youth (*i. e.*, born when parents are young). Happy is the man that hath his quiver full of them, they shall not be ashamed, but they shall speak with the enemy in the gate." (Psalm cxxvii.)

If the secret history of many houses were told, the gentle and soft-sounding words, "providence" and "bereavement," would be stricken out, and the sterner ones, "child-murder" and "suicide," would be put in their place.

However some may think it, a family is not an evil, God has not made it such. It is the most beautiful thing that He has given on the earth. A well ordered Christian family is the most precious thing that the world possesses. Children are *jewels*, and the word is too poor and mean to express the hundredth part of the thought. What more lovely sight is there, what more full of deepest, tenderest interest than a numerous family, one of those large families which you and I have seen, of which perhaps we have been privileged members? And what sight, I add, is more desolate and sad than that of a lonely couple growing old in a lonely home, with neither son nor daughter to support their steps, with no hand to be laid upon their grey heads, going to the grave with the consciousness that their very name perishes with them! Happy they, if they shall be able to say that it was God's appointment, not their own.

The family has its cares and its sorrows, but the cares are a discipline and the sorrows may be sanctified. Like any other good in this fallen world, it carries with it anxieties and burdens which will make traces on the brow and scars upon the heart; but the joys and the comforts are immeasurably above the cares. A Christian family!—who shall tell of its beauty and blessedness? That home where the family altar is, and where God abides, how sweet and hallowed! The family where an affectionate and honored father, a lovely and beloved mother sit with children that sing and laugh around them! Is there a scene in all this wide world like that? It is the nearest to heaven of anything I know; indeed, the Bible takes it as the very symbol of heaven and of the church of Christ, and can give the saints no better name than The Family of God.

Has God given you a family? Look upon it as a great and precious gift, a high and holy trust. Value it somewhat in accordance with its priceless worth, as something which He has put in your hand for the world and for Him. Say not that you can do nothing for your country or your God while you have a child to train or a family under your influence. A well ordered family! Living, you can point to no work like that; dying, you can leave no such legacy behind you.

Remember, too, that earth's changes are evermore going on, and are altering the look of your homes. The little one, yesterday nestling in your arms, to-day with satchel on his arm is shouting home from school; to-morrow he will have gone a bearded man from his old home. And there are broken links in the chain of love, there are vacant chairs, there are empty cradles. Death will not cease his work. Be all and do all that you can there in your home; make it blessed as you may.

I know that as you read there may be sad memories in your heart, and you have almost lost the words as your dimmed eye has been looking into the saddened past. "The old home!—my family!—where are they?" So your bursting heart has been saying. But be not all sad. It is good to know that there is a world where the broken links shall be gathered in one circle again, and where the lost shall be regained.

CHAPTER II.

HUSBANDS AND WIVES: MUTUAL DUTIES.

Wherefore they are no more twain but one flesh.
—MATT. xix. 6.

The kindest and the happiest pair
Will find occasion to forbear;
And something, every day they live,
To pity and perhaps forgive.
COWPER.

IT was not by mere accident that our Lord gave His great announcement of the sacredness of the marriage relation. Just at the moment when the Church of God was to emerge upon a broader field—one not less broad than the whole world over which it should spread—when many rites and ceremonies of a dispensation now grown obsolete were passing away—He, the Son of God, took up the law of marriage as given at the creation, and, with all His great authority, announced its clear, emphatic and perpetual significance.

It is well at times, and especially when, as now, there is much loose talk about the conjugal relation, to turn to the great foundation-truth as given by the Creator and Revealer.

In the Scripture which I have made a motto for this chapter, our Lord asserts the original unity of husband and wife. While they were made different beings, and at different times, yet the one was for the other in such a sense, that, when the marriage was constituted, they ceased to be separate individualities. He asserts that this law of being is to be unchanged. So intimate is the relation established, that it is as if there were now but one common organism between them—" They twain are one flesh."

This remarkable language is repeated by the apostle Paul, and for the purpose of exhibiting, as clearly as possible, a fact upon a right appreciation of which so much of human happiness depends. No words could convey the idea more strongly, for this is the language of hyperbole. The personalities of husband and wife are distinct, but the relation which subsists between them, mentally and spiritually, is so close that it is as if there were no material separation. Thought, feeling, desire, hope, all are consonant and harmonious—they are one.

The marriage relation is as pure and sacred as it is intimate. The Bible everywhere speaks of it in the most exalted terms, and uses it to represent the highest and holiest themes. The union between believers and their Lord is made to resemble it, and the intimate fellowship between Him and His Church is compared to the communion of sympathy and love between a husband and a wife.

As such is the uniform way in which the Bible speaks of this relation, we have not to go far before we reach the idea that the married state is the proper and normal condition of the man and woman. Celibacy is against nature.

I am aware that the opinion of the apostle Paul is often quoted as against the marriage relation; yet I apprehend only from a mistake as to his actual intention and meaning. To prove that his language is not to be interpreted as hostile to the general law and privilege of marriage, it would be only necessary to quote the very numerous and beautiful allusions of Paul himself, and the high and sanctified estimate which he puts upon it, even in these very epistles. Paul himself, according to ancient tradition, which I do not vouch for, had been a married man, but was now a widower, and he preferred to remain such, that he might the more effectually do the work to which he had been called. Without a home, wandering from place to place, constantly suffering privation and exposed to perils of every kind, it was, in his estimation, manifestly improper that he should, to use his own peculiar language, "lead about a wife" (1 Cor. ix. 5). What made him prefer an unmarried state induced him to recommend it to others. *For the present distress, I suppose it is good for a man so to be* (1 Cor. vii. 26), are his words. These early Christians were surrounded by enemies who were ready, at any time, to inflict the most terrible calamities upon them; they were liable to all the evils of poverty, exile and death itself; and Paul's opinion was that he would be most happy upon whom the care of a wife and family did not rest. Yet even while he made this remark, in answer to their inquiries, he is very careful to tell them that it is merely his individual and private opinion and not an authoritative command. Elsewhere he enumerates the "forbidding to marry" as one among the signs which stamped the characters of wicked deceivers in the Church, saying, in energetic language, "Now the Spirit speaketh expressly, that in the latter times some shall depart from the faith, giving heed to *seducing spirits and doctrines of devils*, speaking lies in hypocrisy; having their conscience seared with a hot iron, forbidding to marry," etc. (1 Tim. iv. 1–3); and he expresses his high appreciation of the elevated and honorable relation of husband and wife in the most emphatic terms. It is, indeed, one of the marked peculiarities of the Bible that it everywhere so exalts marriage. There is no book like it in this regard; and, being an Eastern book, this is all the more wonderful.

But nature and the great laws of social intercourse, as ordained by God, regulate this matter with an authority and power higher than all the reasonings or arrangements of man. Mutual affection, having a heavenly birth, and going out from souls made for each other, will not be satisfied till it has found its proper home and rest in the married state. "Here," says Jeremy Taylor, "is the proper scene of piety and patience, of the duty of parents and the charity of relatives; here kindness is spread abroad, and love is united and made firm as a centre; marriage is the nursery of heaven; the virgin sends prayers to God, but she carries but one soul to Him; but the state of marriage fills up the numbers of the elect, and hath in it the labor of love and the delicacies of friendship, the blessing of society and the union of hands and hearts; it hath in it less of beauty but more of safety than single life; it hath more care but less danger; it is more merry and more sad; it is fuller of sorrows and fuller of joys; it lies under more burdens, but is supported by all the strength of love and charity, and those burdens are delightful." Here manhood finds its proper development. Indeed, there is no real development of the man without it. "That man," says one of the old Jewish writers, "whomsoever he be, that hath no wife, is the least of a man," and with show of correctness. In the original creation of man, as if to exhibit impressively this truth, he was first made and left alone.

Then, when the animate creation had been searched for a companion and none was found, the woman was made, because it was "not good that the man should be alone." There were necessities of his nature which could only be met by a sympathetic soul, and that the soul of not another man but of a woman and a wife. A character, however excellent outside this state, is always imperfect and needs some elements which can only be developed there to round it into completeness and symmetry. Of this the thoughtful and considerate celibate himself is conscious.

I will not be deemed guilty of the absurdity of here asserting that marriage does, of necessity, create perfect characters. There are some men whom not even the society of a wife and the holy companionships of marriage can make much better than brutes; of such the question is—what would they have been without these softening influences?

But the design and the true tendency of marriage is to call out the deeper and better elements of man's nature, to tone down the harsher, to mellow the harder, to introduce him into a world of sympathies and emotions to which otherwise he would be altogether a stranger.

As I have just said, marriage is not sufficient in itself to make a man, so I would be as far from seeming to assert that no strong and manly, no sweet and beautiful characters are found outside this relation. There are men and women who, like some flowers, bloom in exquisite beauty in a desert wild; they are like trees which you often see growing in luxuriant strength out of a crevice of a rock where there seems not earth enough to support a shrub. The words "Old maid," "Old bachelor," have in them other sounds than that of half reproach or scorn; they call up to many of your minds forms and faces than which none are dearer in all this world. I know them to-day. The bloom of youth has possibly faded from their cheeks, but there lingers round form and face something dearer than that. She is unmarried, but the past has, for her, it may be, some chastened memories of an early love which keeps its vestal vigil sleeplessly over the grave where its hopes went out; and it is too true to the long-departed to permit another to take his place. Perhaps the years of maiden life were spent in self-denying toil, which was too engrossing to listen even to the call of love, and she grew old too soon in the care of mother or sister and brother. Now in these later years she looks back calmly upon some half-cherished hopes, once attractive, of husband and child, but which long, long ago she willingly gave up for present duty. So to-day, in her loneness, who shall say that she is not beautiful and dear?

So is she to the wide circle which she blesses. To some she has been all that a mother could have been; and though no nearer name than "Aunt" or "Sister" has been hers, she has to-day a mother's claim and a mother's love. Disappointment has not soured but only chastened; the midday or the afternoon of her life is all full of kindly sympathies and gentle deeds. Though unwedded, hers has been no fruitless life.

It is an almost daily wonder to me why some women are married, and not a less marvel why many that I see are not. But this I know, that many and many a household would be desolate indeed, and many and many a family circle would lose its brightest ornament and its best power, were maiden sister or maiden aunt removed, and it may bless the Providence which has kept them from making glad some husband's home.

Yonder isolated man, whom the world wonder at for having never found a wife! who shall tell you all the secret history of the by-gone time! of hopes and loves that once were buoyant and fond, but which death, or more bitter disappointment dashed to the ground; of sorrow which the world has never known; of a fate accepted in utter despair, though with outward calm! Such there are. The expectation of wife, or home, has been given up as one of the dreams of youth, but only with groans and tears; now he walks among men somewhat alone, with some eccentricities, but with a warm heart and kindly eye. If he has no children of his own, there are enough of others' children who climb his knee or seize his hand as he walks. If he has no home, there is many a home made glad by his presence; if there is no one heart to which he may cling in appropriating love, there are many hearts that go out toward him, and many voices which invoke benedictions on his head.

I might say more, but I could not say less of a class that I love to think of as holding a place made for them in God's providence, and filling it with honor to themselves and with beneficence for others.

The marriage-day is the entrance upon a new world; the husband and wife, hand in hand, like happy voyagers, have stepped on a shore which henceforth is to be their future home. There is no return; the boat which carried them has been burned upon the beach, and for better or for worse they are to abide in the new land. Whether their future shall be happy or miserable will depend wholly upon the way in which they shall discharge the duties inseparable from the relation in which they stand to one another.

One of the first of these duties is *a cultivation of unity of feeling.* The theory of married life is that the parties are *one:* "They twain shall be one flesh." But too often it is a theory only, and never a practical reality. They are brought, it is true, on the nuptial day more closely, indeed inexorably together; they live in the most intimate associations possible; but there may be, at the same time, an entire absence of that *unity of spirit* which constitutes the inner truth of marriage. Each may be moving in an entirely different hemisphere of thought and feeling, and a wide ocean may keep them apart.

Between a husband and wife there can be no separated interests. Property, reputation, happiness belong to them both without the possibility that the one should be touched and the other not feel. The circle which bounds the place where they stand side by side, is too small for any cloud or any patch of sunshine to throw shadow or gleam upon one and not the other.

So important did this sentiment of unity between a husband and wife seem among Romans of the earlier time, that, it is said, even gifts were forbidden between them. They would not permit the delicacy of the sentiment to be hazarded by anything, even though it should come in the way of a token of affection. It was as if it were an absurdity for one to make a present to himself; his wife was himself.

While this was pushing the idea beyond its proper bounds, yet it is certain that nothing should be neglected which shall keep in full activity this feeling of unity. The moment the thought is allowed that there is any diversity of interest, that moment a foundation is laid of distrust and estrangement.

There should be *no secrets between a husband and wife.* From the hour that they are such to each other, there ceases to be any occasion for secrecy. What is there which one shall conceal from himself? and if not from himself, why from his wife? What is there that a wife ought to possess that she cannot make her husband a sharer in? There is an inner sanctuary in which they two alone abide; no other being in all the world has right to enter there, and neither husband nor wife has right to bring another in! The secret that is imparted to a wife under the pledge that her husband shall not know it, is a secret which she ought not to receive. What a husband promises not to reveal to his wife is usually what he should not know. I speak in general terms. There may be cases (seldom, I think,) when a secret is of such a nature, and involves the interests of others in such a manner, that it may rightly be kept from even one so near. But what I insist on is this, that nothing should be allowed to interrupt, for an hour, the sense of absolute union—nothing to come in and push apart the souls that intermingle here. A thing concealed will do it.

This one idea, as you perceive, sweeps over a large extent, and might give us subject for a whole chapter in itself. It touches all the companionships, the habits, the associations, the thoughts, the feelings that either may cherish. If they are thus absolutely one, and the unity is cherished, they can have no separate friends; neither can have companions, associations, or habits that the other repudiates. I know that this insisted on will narrow the circle in which wife or husband moves; it will cause some to drop away; it will prevent your hearing many a bit of gossip; will make you lose more than one piece of scandal; it may, possibly, prevent your having any of those "intimate and confidential friends" which some like to talk of; but, be assured, it will make your married life none the less happy on that account.

To persons who understand this fully, there will be a sense of oppression in having something on the mind of which they cannot speak to husband or wife, and rather than submit to this feeling they will forego the knowledge which is offered them. "She will be sure to tell her husband," "He will go home and let his wife know it":—these may seem words of reproach, but they are, in reality, an encomium on the transparent medium which is between those united hearts.

I need scarcely say that where this unity is felt and understood there will be no such thing as talking unfavorably of each other. For a wife to permit to escape her lips, so that it reaches the ear of a third person, a complaint against her husband, to expose his faults or give utterance to her grievances, is to do a foolish and usually a wicked thing; for a husband openly to censure his wife, to speak of her habits or her acts so that others shall think less respectfully of her, is to proclaim his own shame; they both tell the world that, whatever they may be in name, they are no longer one in heart. It is fortunate that the common sense of men hold this in scorn. If there are causes of complaint or grounds of difficulty, they are to be settled between themselves alone. No third person can or ought to come in; to even *ask the advice* of a third person is to give evidence that the identity of the married life has gone.

Another thing which lies at the foundation of happiness in married life, is—*The duty of understanding one another.* In this world, more than half the quarrels which afflict men are caused by *misunderstandings.* It would seem, at first glance, that where two stand so closely related to one another, each must, of necessity, be fully cognizant of what the other is. Yet it is pitiable to see how utterly a husband and a wife may be ignorant of the first elements of each other's characters, and how this ignorance makes their life one perpetual misadaptation. For even though intention be never so good, how can one adapt himself or his acts to the feelings or the thoughts which he misunderstands or falsely interprets? One of the first duties, then, is for the parties *to know each other;* and this will not be difficult where both have the one end—mutual happiness in view. They should study each other's characters, or rather find them out by that subtle power which love has when it seeks to promote the well-being of another. The true wife may not be able to tell you, in words, all about her husband's peculiarities; but she has a wonderfully quick way of adapting herself to them, and she does it so perfectly that he, possibly she herself, does not think it an adaptation, only a natural act that could hardly have been done differently. An appreciative husband orders his words, his movements, his life, so that the quick sensibilities of a sensitive wife are so delicately met that they vibrate only tunefully. Every one has some peculiarity of disposition or temperament. These are what make individuality. The wise husband and wife find them quickly out, and, like skillful musicians, pitch the music of their life by them.

Let me not be told by some married one that his wife is so nervous and fretful and discontented that she cannot be made happy, or by some wife that her husband is so morose and fault-finding that nothing will please him. Good Sir Thomas Browne says (*Religio Medici*): "Methinks there is no man bad, and the worst best, that is while they are kept within the circle of those qualities wherein they are good; there is no man's mind of such discordant and jarring a temper to which a tunable disposition may not strike harmony." The two grand requisites are: first the knowledge of the key, and then this tunable disposition. When these are present there will be no lack of harmony in the house.

Another of these mutual duties is *Forbearance with each other*. Happy are they to whom marriage brings no unwelcome revelations. There is a veil of beauty and romance hanging over the days of courtship and early marriage, like the thin mists which make the landscape lovely in autumn time. In these halcyon days each appears to the other in the most attractive form, not only of character, but of outward garb. The instinct is to be seen not more with smiles than with well arrranged hair or pleasing dress. The unlovely traits of character are concealed, not by art, but out of love. Love allows no opportunity in the brief and too quickly passing hours of that dreamy time for anything but the beautiful to appear.

But sooner or later these days are over, and the veil drops of itself away. Anticipated joys have become realities; the interrupted moments of courtship have given place to permanent possession and continued residence together. Now begins the work of revealment, of which I have spoken, and it is not strange if things are learned that are neither beautiful nor lovely. Often these discoveries are fatal. Because the husband is not the exalted being that he once seemed, because the wife has found him to be after all only a man, and not a very noble one, with some habits that she abhors, and much that she cannot admire; because the husband does not find his wife that sweet ethereal creature, all smiles and gentleness, that he imagined, but very prosaic and sometimes waspish, they turn away from each other in mutual disgust and disappointment. This is the end of all their happiness. Henceforth married life is a slavery, whose chains fret and gall; and death, if it comes soon enough, is a welcome manumission.

There are few, perhaps none, who have not made some such unwelcome discovery, and had such sober experience when the Indian-summer of the honey-moon has passed and chilly autumnal days have come. Now is the time when the happiness of future life is at stake; if they yield to the impressions, and sullenly determine that while they may be chained indissolubly together, yet they can never have any thing in common, then dreary indeed will be the coming time, all the more dismal because of the hopes, now dead, which ushered it in. But if they wisely look at these discoveries, as not only inevitable, but to be expected, and determine in a spirit of love to make the best of them, all will be well, and the years of married life will only draw their hearts closer together. Some early dreams may have been dissipated, but they will appear only foolish dreams; a calmer and a deeper reality of love has succeeded; husband and wife are better now than even in the vague thoughts of other days.

Let the newly married make up their minds that they will find out much that they do not know at first, and that it will not be all good to see, but let them at the same time resolve to make the best of all they learn of each other. If your husband is not all that you picture him, remember that you are not the angel you once appeared; if your wife is more ungraceful in faded calico than in lace-trimmed silk, and more tart in temper now than when you saw her for an hour or two on her good behavior, do not forget that you in your uncoated sleeves, unwashed face, and possibly not sunny humor, are not the noble being she took you to be. You have both something to bear as well as to enjoy, and the bearing will make the enjoying:

> "Oh, we do all offend—
> There's not a day of wedded life, if we
> Count at its close the little, bitter sum
> Of thoughts, and words, and looks unkind and froward—
> Silence that chides, and woundings of the eye—
> But prostrate at each other's feet, we should
> Each night forgiveness ask."

While the poet, one would hope, has given us a sadly overdrawn picture, yet no stream flows so smoothly but that somewhere on its surface a ripple appears, and no married life but that here and there a moment of discord disturbs its calm serenity.

I have seen a story somewhere of Dr. Samuel Johnson. A good-natured lady was expatiating on the happiness of her married life, and said, enthusiastically and exultantly: "Why, doctor, we have lived together twenty years and have never had a disagreement." The great bear looked half scornfully down and simply said, "Madam, how insipid!" While I would not, perhaps, wholly endorse the doctor's opinion, yet I am satisfied that two human beings who have not yet become perfect, cannot be perpetually together without sometimes thinking differently and willing in opposition to one another. I know that there are here and there a husband and wife who are conscious of no such opposition, who can look back over, possibly, years of uninterrupted communings and undivided purposes, and who might easily suppose that it is because they are always the same in thought and purpose. But, I take it, it is rather that, impelled by a mutual affection and a keen-sighted wisdom, they have unconsciously learned to allow nothing for a moment to stand between their hearts.

To accomplish this, a husband and wife must *Guard against the beginning of estrangemeut.* The lasting alienations, the separations, the divorces do not spring at once out of some great violations of conjugal duty, but are the perfected fruit of little estrangements. A word or a look, sometimes, like a small break in a dyke, becomes a vast crevasse, through which pours a flood of unhappiness. Nay, it may be that a positive nothing, only a fancied neglect, becomes the far-reaching cause of untold misery. It is noticed and felt, but pride forbids any explanation or any questioning. Each feels the other's coldness, but neither can come to the point of asking what is in the way. Meanwhile the peaceful current of mutual agreement is broken up; the stream is turbid and frets its banks. Each is unhappy, and, I may say, each is conscious of wrong. In this state of mind, a new offence is easily given, and more easily taken, and the breach grows wider and wider. The process may go on till wife or husband, perhaps both, begin to seek in the society of others what they have lost in their own, and, at last, embarked on a troubled and rapid stream, in some dark hour they are hurried into crime, and are lost to each other forever.

"A something, light as air—a look,
  A word unkind or wrongly taken—
Oh! love, that tempests never shook,
  A breath, a touch like this has shaken.
And ruder winds will soon rush in,
To spread the breach that words begin;
And eyes forget the gentle ray
They wore in courtship's smiling day;
And voices lose the tone that shed
A tenderness round all they said;

Till fast declining, one by one
The sweetnesses of love are gone,
And hearts, so lately mingled, seem
Like broken clouds—or like the stream
That smiling left the mountain's brow,
  As though its waters ne'er could sever,
Yet ere it reached the plain below,
  Breaks into floods and parts forever."

But where alienation does not go to such fearful lengths, how many and many an hour of bitter unhappiness is passed, especially by a newly-wedded pair, in misery, caused by some petty thing which should not have interrupted their happiness a moment. How many a hot tear has flowed, how many a heartache has been suffered in secret, when a single word, perhaps a look, an arm thrown round the neck, a kiss given, might in a moment have swept every cloud away and brought back sunshine and joy to the home! Let, then, the husband and wife beware of little things.

But if these little offences, or even greater ones, have been given or taken, no moment should be allowed to pass before a reconciliation is effected. Let both resolve, that, under no circumstances, and for no reason, will they permit a cloud to intervene between them, or obscure the sunshine of their wedded life.

Some will read this who understand me fully, and have known too many days of misery not to appreciate what I say. If you are conscious, and as soon as you are conscious, that there is anything of alienation or estrangement, lose not an hour before you seek a reunion of your hearts. If conscience tells you that you have been in the wrong, do not be too proud to acknowledge it; if you are sure that you have been unkindly or unjustly treated, do not stand on your dignity or sense of justice, but be the first to seek a reconciliation. Let the magnanimity of love move you. Do not wait till your husband or your wife approaches you, but do you hasten to do love's work. You will find, perhaps, another heart reaching out after your's in the dark, and it will not be long before you both are walking side by side and hand clasped in hand.

A deeper tone, and a sweeter, would be given usually to the married life, if husbands and wives would be more demonstrative and be willing to give expression to their affection. I do not mean, now, in the often empty and vapid "my dear," or " my love," which make up a common mode of address. The words are often full of sweet meaning, but they come glibly, too, from those who, if they had spoken out of their heart, would have used very different terms. Perhaps these would have been—" My torment," " my disgust;" and sometimes they are the most frequent when in secret the alienation is widest, a sort of vane telling you that a northeast wind is blowing. I mean that husbands and wives should be in the habit of giving visible expression to their feelings. A mother does not hesitate to embrace her child or imprint kisses on his cheek; a father is not ashamed to take his daughter on his knee even though she be grown; and why should they, whose union is nearer, never give outward form to what glows within?

There are those who not only never before others give any signs of affection, but who never show it even in the sanctuary of their own inner life. It should not be so. If you have love to one another, show it; it is sacred and pure and precious enough only to be gloried in.

Read the Bible and pray with each other. To a Christian husband and wife, I trust, little need be said upon this topic, and especially to those who have a family about them. How a father and a mother, who pretend to hope that they have any religion at all, can consent to be without family worship it is difficult to understand. To have a family from God and yet never to acknowledge God in the family; to receive hourly the untold family blessings and have no family religion, is something which would seem to lie simply outside the circle of ordinary Christian thought. But if there are no children given you, as two believers in Christ, bound so intimately together, you ought to have that union cemented daily by God's word and the sacrifice of prayer and praise; you should stand hand in hand beside one altar, and not be offering only separate and isolated offerings. A wife's sweet voice in prayer—and it is never sweeter than then—should be to her husband's ear as familiar a sound as is his to her.

But I refer in this remark to every husband and wife, whether they are professors of religion or not. Prayer is nothing to be ashamed of, and you ought not to be startled if, while you are kneeling before God, your companion should come suddenly upon you. It will be beautiful and sweet if, at such a time, you are conscious, though, with closed eyes, that a dear form has softly knelt by your side. But more than this, be in the habit of praying together.

> "Together should our prayers ascend;
> Together should we humbly bend,
> To praise the Almighty name."

Yes, you have too many mercies to praise Him for; were there nothing else, the love which makes your life radiant for each other may give you inspiration; you have too many common hopes and fears, forebodings and expectations; too many common wants; you are too much to each other never to go before your Heavenly Father hand in hand.

I could relate stories of deep and tender interest to illustrate what I am writing of, and some will read this whose eyes will, perhaps, grow dim with tears of grateful recollection as they are reminded of by-gone scenes in their own history, which are of all the sweetest and the tenderest.

Though you have never joined the church or outwardly professed to be Christians, yet bring the hallowed atmosphere of prayer and of God's holy word over your married life. Kneel together, and, in turn, from night to night lift up your hearts to God. Oh, you cannot tell what a depth, what a purity, what a profound joyousness it will give your love. And, I may add, it will have in it the germ of blessings greater than you now imagine.

CHAPTER III.

HUSBANDS.

Husbands love your wives, even as Christ also loved the church, and gave Himself for it.—Ephes. v. 25.

I wonder did you ever count
  The value of one human fate:
Or scan the infinite amount
  Of one heart's treasures, and the weight
Of Life's one venture, and the whole
  Concentrate purpose of a soul:

And if you ever paused to think
  That all this in your hands I laid
Without a fear: did you not shrink
  From such a burden, half afraid,
    Half wishing that you could divide
  The risk or cast it all aside?

Adelaide Proctor.

THERE is something startling in the way in which that passage in the Epistle of Paul speaks of a husband's love. It is to be nothing short of that divine love which the Lord of Glory had to the Church which he died to redeem.

What abysses of holy, self-sacrificing affection are here! Into what a temple he enters who takes the hand of a woman and leads her away from all the world beside, to the inner shrine of marriage!

In the absolute surrender of the wife to her husband, and the completeness of the abandonment of her well-being to his hands, there is that which makes the highest possible standard and the clearest and most emphatic call for love. When you look at it thoughtfully, there is an element of presumption in a man's asking a woman to become his wife, or asking a daughter at the hands of her parents. Consider it. Here is a man asking a woman whose life and whose happiness are as valuable as his own, to give that life and happiness into his keeping. He asks that she shall give up all her former friends and associations, at least subordinate them wholly—and usually it is a total forsaking of them—to the friends and associations to which he shall bring her; that she shall leave the protection of her father and mother and brothers; leave her old home, it may be, the happy home of her childhood, and commit herself to the keeping of a comparative stranger;

not only to put herself under his sole protection, but to give herself wholly to him, trusting all that has any value to his care.

Now, I say, when you look at it in this light, he must be a bold and reckless man, or else one impelled by the self-confidence of love who can ask all this without a half consciousness of temerity.

The wife does literally leave all, and from her marriage-day deliver over all into the hands of her husband. She goes out from the paternal door, and it is only the outward sign that she has exchanged father and brothers, her many natural protectors for one other. Marriage inevitably breaks up the old friendships. However a wife may desire to hold them and keep up the old loves, they do naturally, and by a fatal necessity, die away; not, perhaps, at once, but gradually and gently, like the fading notes of a sweet song. The circle will change its circumference as its centre has changed; taking in its sweep new sympathies, it will leave out the old. Others are conscious of this even before the bride herself. How often an old and cherished friend, who seemed to hold a place so near to her heart that neither time nor space could ever separate them, has been filled with sadness and surprise at the gulf which a day of married life has put between them. I have known an old school-mate look in undisguised wonder at her friend, gazing to see what had made the strange transformation and removed her so utterly and so soon away from her side. But the removal has been made. The separation is final and complete; the old familiar intimacy can never, I may add, ought never be renewed. Nor is this surprising. It is only in accordance with the great and unalterable law of marriage. The wife has forsaken all, given herself wholly to her husband, and her life and her thoughts take their shape from the fact.

The husband then receives into his care the well-being of one who has given up all for him, a whole world of affectionate sympathies, of tremulous emotions, of hopes, of fears, of desires and aspirations; there clings one to him who looks upward expecting all from his love.

The reception of such a trust brings with it responsibilities and duties.

The fact is very evident that the wife leaves all for her husband, and we are so ready to look upon this as a well known and well understood duty, that possibly it would create a surprise in many minds were I to say that I know of no text in the New Testament where the wife is commanded to leave those who are near to her for her husband; the Scriptures which refer to the matter are in all cases directed to the husband: "For this cause shall *a man* leave his father and mother and be joined unto his wife." The direction and the explicitness of the command indicate where the chief danger lay, and who in this relation needed the admonition most. The husband, by the fact of his life being more abroad, and possibly by reason of other influences, is more exposed to temptation to unfaithfulness. The surrender on his part is as absolute and perfect as on hers; he in the act of marriage at once and forever forsakes all others for her. On his fidelity depends all her earthly happiness, nay, it exists at all only as that fidelity stands without a shadow over its calm brilliancy. If such be the case, then a husband should give occasion not for an instant to a suspicion that another is attracting a thought, least of all an affection. I do not now speak of the wretch who could be false to his marriage vow, but of that thoughtless trifling with the deepest and best feelings of a woman's nature, of which some husbands make so light. She has a right to claim all her husband's heart, and to have it appear to all the world that she has it. Yet some men, while they do not intend deliberately a wrong, show attentions of such a marked character that they cannot but be observed as indicative of the fact that another has come in and is at least sharing the domain of the wife: then if a cloud is seen coming over the wife's brow, he speaks perhaps of "foolish jealousy." But it is not foolish jealousy. A wife ought to be able to lean against his bosom and say with joyous confidence: "I am reigning here alone," and the assurance shall be as a diadem on the husband's brow.

One of the first duties of a husband is *to sympathize with his wife.* While the two are so closely and intimately connected with each other, they do not move within the same sphere; they have surroundings very different. The wife has duties and cares which are peculiarly hers, and they are as engrossing and exhaustive as his. He has the responsibilities, the anxieties, the perplexities of business; she has the not less weighty charge of the household. Many a man seems to regard these household duties of the wife as not to be compared for a moment with those which engross his attention. He expects, if business has perplexed or made him anxious, to have his wife's sympathy when he comes home at night, but never imagines that during the day any thing could have occurred to trouble that wife. He returns from his workshop or counting-room soured, perhaps, by some bad bargain, annoyed by a stupid workman or unreasonable employer, morose from some ill-spoken word, and expects to be received with smiles; it matters not how surly may be *his* looks, his wife must be in dress, in countenance, in word, all sweetness and amiability. He may have no pleasant word, may take his place moodily at his table, but his wife's words must be affectionate, and his wife's looks full only of gladness. What, he thinks, has she to trouble her? And this when the poor wife has through a long and weary day been toiling with family work and vexatious care till her head is aching and foot and hand and heart are sore with the worry. The tea is dispatched silently, very likely with sombre complaints over the trials he has had during the day, or the badness of the times; and then the evening paper is taken in hand and pored over until the very advertisements are devoured, or the reader's face is bowed upon the crumpled page in sleep. Or, if he be not weary enough for that, he seizes his hat and rushes for the reading-room, or more probably for the lounging-place where such as he do congregate; there, with a fragment of segar in his hand and desultory talk from his lips, he lingers till the noise of the closing shutters warns him to leave. He goes at last home again, because he can go nowhere else. Meanwhile the wife has with heavy heart and tired step got the little ones into bed, and, as best she could, has worn away the long hours of the evening in silence and loneliness. Should a thought of his selfishness or injustice cross the mind of the husband, he responds with ready self-complacency, "I require relaxation and must see my friends." The night is witness of the same or greater lack of sympathy. Perhaps the babe is not well and is restless. But that is not his business. It matters not that the poor pale wife has had the child in her arms through the long day—

a day's work with a sick babe, one of the weariest of mortal toils—he must not be disturbed. I have known such a husband provide a distant sleeping apartment that he might not be disturbed, and lie snoring in leaden unconsciousness while a frail wife, with swollen eyes, and limbs that almost refused to obey an iron will, was walking to and fro with his child.

In the morning he expects to find his breakfast ready on the moment of his call, the coffee clear, if his temper is not, and his wife smiling and pleasant, though he is dull or bearish. Perhaps he never notices the pale face or swollen eyelid, the result of last night's watching, part of it simply to keep his slumbers undisturbed, lest his impatience should be added to his sick child's crying. If he does notice them, it is only to wonder at the "delicacy of our women"—"they can stand but little"—"if she only had my work to do!" Probably, however, he does not notice them. He goes soon to his business, without a word of sympathy or interest, and leaves her to another lonely day and its thousand great and petty trials, as if he had nothing whatever to do with them.

Now this is all wrong. No manly husband

should be guilty of it. He has no right thus to separate himself from the labors and responsibilities of his wife. If he does not actually relieve them by his help, he can at least sympathize with her and aid her by kind words and pleasant looks. Many a sad wife would feel more than compensated for all the toils of a vexatious day by a word which showed that her husband understood her cares and felt with her in them. And I apprehend in many an instance the help would be beyond mere words; the sympathetic husband would not be deterred by the lazy and selfish excuse—"It is woman's work," but would uplift part of the burden, and possibly take his turn in watching, and give or provide relief from household drudgery. At all events, a husband that loves somewhat after the Bible rule, thoughtfully considers and warmly sympathizes with his wife in all her cares.

A true sympathy and conjugal intimacy will lead to the performance of what I consider another duty of a husband:—

Consultation with his wife. There are many men who seem to consider their wives as capable of understanding nothing but what relates to dress or cooking, and they would smile at the folly of talking with them on any matter which relates to business. I am aware that there are women of whom it would be folly to make confidants in such things; women who are reckless and thoughtless enough to urge their husbands into all sorts of extravagance, that their pride and vanity may be gratified, regardless wholly of results, and who would pettishly refuse to listen to any explanation of business affairs; yet I think even such would be far fewer, if, from the first, husbands were accustomed to confide to them their plans and to seek their advice. Almost the poorest wife could be trained to interest in them, and could be made a helper. If a wife be always treated as not fit to know any thing of her husband's affairs, if her questions receive only cold and half scornful replies, it is not to be wondered at if she soon ceases to feel any interest, or have any thoughts about them; and if, by and by, it should be found in a practical way that she does not seem to "know much of the value of money," or "how much it costs to get it," or even "where it comes from," the reticent husband need not wonder.

A man who understands this matter will avail himself of his wife's help, even in his business affairs. The intuitions of a woman are better and readier than those of a man; her quick decisions without reasons are frequently far superior to a man's most careful deductions. He is a wise husband who makes use of his wife's shrewdness and womanly sagacity, the fruits of this faculty. Many and many a man would have been saved from ruin had he consulted his wife and acted upon her advice before he embarked in his enterprizes. And how often would a husband find almost all the bitterness taken out of his reverses, did he bring his wife's powerful aid to help him through them.

Let me say, then, to every husband: Make a confidant of your wife; show her that you respect her abilities and are glad to avail yourself of them. You will find that she grows under the culture of confidence. Be accustomed to tell her of your schemes and purposes; if disaster and trouble threaten, do not conceal them, rather frankly let her know them. No man appreciates the value of his wife until he has tested her counsel and sympathy. These you cannot afford to be without. Consult your wife. You will honor and love her the more, and you will find her respecting and clinging to you with a more intelligent affection.

Another duty of a husband is to *show affection.* The duty of a man to love his wife is too palpable for the necessity of lingering upon it. The injunction of God's holy word with its great illustration — "Husbands, love your wives as Christ loved the Church"—and the very idea of marriage are enough. Marriage without love is the most dreadful of all bondages. For two persons who do not love each other, to be bound in this intimate relation, where every thing has its significance only as explained by true affection, where all, without it, degenerates at once into the lowest and basest; to be called husband and wife with none of the sweet intimacies of the soul, the pure communings of heart, the all-yielding confidence of marriage: — that is to drink, it seems to me, life's bitterest cup; it is to have lost all, next to religion, that life is worth living for.

But while all readily see the necessity of love in marriage, the duty of *manifesting* it is not so generally understood. In my last chapter I spoke of this as equally incumbent on husband and wife. I wish now to speak of it as especially the duty of the husband, for I am of the opinion that we are in more danger of neglecting it than our wives. There are very few women who would not respond to evidences of affection, who would not return a caress of their husbands; but there are many men who would not only not notice them from their wives, but would soon, by their indifference, make it certain that these tokens of love would never be offered.

A husband may be affectionate—I confess that I do not understand exactly how it can be, but I suppose it may be so—without manifesting it by any outward signs; but what I wish to insist on is that the love ought to be shown out *in act and words*. There are, I know, differences of temperament; and it would be folly to look for the same expression of affection from every one. There is a striking difference in the way in which children will show attachment. Some persons are more demonstrative than others, and with, perhaps, not as much of true love, will appear to have vastly more than others who make less show of it. But I am of the opinion that where it actually exists, at all, it will and must find some expression. For myself I find it difficult to believe in the existence of that which gives no sign of life. "Nothing," says a living writer, speaking on another topic, "can live which is not permitted to show signs of life. Even a tree, a solid, massive oak, embracing the earth in roots equal to half its volume, and drawing out of the rich soil its needed nutriment, will be stifled and yield up its life if it cannot put on leaves at the extremities and grow." In the dawn of married life, and especially in the days of courtship, when the lover was wooing his bride, his affection had no difficulty in finding modes to exhibit itself; indeed, it found them naturally and without an effort. Its very power consisted in the fact that it was not exhibited, but exhibited itself; it was there; and like "ointment in the hand," it betrayed itself. What was true then, must be equally true in the after times. Do not tell me that the man is soberer, now that the lover has been changed into the husband, and that he cannot be expected to make the same demonstrations of his love. Why not, I ask? Is the wife any less dear now than she was then, before she was his wife? If so, I have nothing to say except to express my pity and sorrow for him and for her. But if with lapse of months and years she has grown upon his heart and fills it more fully than in that earlier time, why shall not that deeper affection find utterance? It will wherever it exists; it will speak in words; it will shine in looks; it will be mirrored in acts.

But when I speak of exhibitions of affection, I do not mean that a husband shall be always using terms of endearment. Nor do I mean that a husband should be endeavoring to demonstrate his affection in some notable way, as for instance by a costly present or the like. No, these may be given, and yet after all an aching heart may sigh for something better.

When I say affection should be exhibited in word and act, I mean those words and acts which spring naturally from a loving heart. It was not terms of endearment or costly gifts which first won the maiden's heart; no, in those early days the one would have been resented and the other refused; but it was tones of the voice, words of interest, all the more dear because half-unconsciously spoken; expressions of thoughtful care or solicitude, given you scarcely knew how; a little flower plucked—it is now faded, but dearer after the lapse of years than gems;—a shawl gathered round the shoulders; a cushion adjusted so that you could rest more comfortably; these were the attractive things, and these are the things, not all remembered now one by one, but which together throw a sweet and hallowed radiance over the time. These are the things which have evermore an untold charm about them.

By the common consent of men, almost any husband would venture his life to save his wife's life from flood or fire, but that would be only some great occasion, probably never to occur in most men's lives; but to show every day those small anticipations of a wife's wishes and little thoughtful attentions, is to give a greater as well as perpetual proof of love. The one is a hurricane which displays sudden, impulsive power; the other is a sweet and all-surrounding atmosphere of life and love.

It is sadly too often the case that these little but mighty things all gradually pass away with the early days of married life. The husband speaks in tones and in language which if uttered in his courtship days would have soon cut them ingloriously short; he is guilty of acts of impoliteness or perpetrates neglects which then would have made certain that the lover would never there get a wife. He who once was all sweetness, whose tones were gentle and kind, whose looks were sympathy, and acts affection, now that a wife is bound indissolubly to him, becomes cold, abrupt, and coarse. Or what, if possible, is worse, he speaks and acts toward his wife as if she of all women were the only one to whom he need not be civil. He addresses her and acts toward her in a way for which, if it were toward any other woman who had a natural protector, he would expect to be rigorously held to account. As she is his wife, he can be brutish with impunity. To such a level as this, no man of high or honorable spirit will ever suffer himself to sink.

A husband should be careful to maintain all that he ever exhibited of thoughtful affection. He should be *polite* to his wife. Because she is your wife, is no reason why you should be attentive to all others and not to her; why you should hastily rise and find a seat for another woman, when you sit still and leave her to provide for herself; or why you should feel at liberty to snub her with some ill-natured or scornful remark. You need not, because she is your wife, avoid taking a quiet walk with her, or be ashamed for the same reason to have her on your arm in the street or the parlor. Rather, and all the more because she is your wife, speak pleasant sympathetic words; show little attentions; give kind and affectionate looks. You may not be able to provide magnificent gifts, jewels and brocades, but you will give what is pricelessly beyond them. Do not be ashamed to hold the hand of your wife, its touch once sent a thrill through your bosom, and you may hold it gently now with a deeper meaning in it; do not blush to imprint a kiss upon her brow, it may not be as fair as then, but the soul within is fairer. Oh, if I could but persuade some men to break through the thick ice of their daily life, and show a little of the love which ought to be in their hearts, I know that there would be upturned faces filled with glad surprise; there would be sad eyes suddenly filled with joyous tears, and white arms that would reach out with an embrace which they have not known in many a year.

Remember that it is not enough that you provide for your family, that your wife is furnished with money, and that you do not treat her unkindly, that you are faithful to her; she has affections that crave something more, and which if not met from you will pine and be all desolate. You may not feel the want, hurried as you are with business care and outward employments, and your nature does not ask it with such deep longings. Of her it has been beautifully said by Longfellow:

> "The world of affections is thy world—
> Not that of man's ambition. In that stillness,
> Which most becomes a woman, calm and holy,
> Thou sittest by the fireside of the heart,
> Feeding its flame."

You may give your wife everything else, but if you do not give your love in such shape that it can be recognized, you have left her only poor.

Here is something for which your wife cannot ask. She can tell you of other wants, that are not to be thought of in comparison with this; but she cannot tell you that she longs for tokens of affection. You must recognize the longing and answer the unuttered call of love.

Never permit the fire of love to go out, and never cease to show that it is burning still.

If any husband that reads this has permitted the flame to burn low on that altar, straightway kindle it up again, and let its fragrant incense be like that which never ceased to rise in Israel's tabernacle. Do not let time or familiarity blunt the fine edge of your affections, or carelessness or habit lead you to neglect those little but all-powerful and sweet attentions which hallow and make beautiful the intimacy of kindred souls. There is a love, an abiding love that survives the decay of beauty, which grows deeper and stronger as the bloom fades from the cheek and the silver streaks the hair, that sings—

> "Say, shall I love the fading beauty less,
> Whose spring-tide radiance has been wholly mine?
> No; come what will, thy steadfast truth I'll bless;
> In youth, in age, thine own—forever thine."

There is a beauty in the young dawn of love, when, in life's morning, two that were just now children are walking with interwined embrace; there is a deeper beauty in the hallowed evidences of affection which light up the home of wedded life, where the man and the woman of riper years have seen days of joy and grief; but there is a golden sunset beauty, almost like the pure light of heaven, that lingers round the path of an aged pair, clinging fondly to one another, when the journey of life is almost over. If there is anything more exquisite in its touching beauty than the picture which Burns draws, I do not know it—

"John Anderson, my jo, John, ye were my first conceit;
And ye na think it strange, John, tho' I ca' ye trim and neat;
Tho' some folk say ye're auld, John, I never think ye so,
But I think ye're ay the same to me, John Anderson, my jo.

"John Anderson, my jo, John, we've seen our bairns' bairns,
And yet my dear John Anderson, I'm happy in your arms;
And sae are ye in mine,—I'm sure ye'll ne'er say no,—
Though the days are gane that we have seen, John Anderson, my jo.

"John Anderson, my jo, John, we clam the hill thegither,
And mony a canty day, John, we've had wi' ane anither;
Now we maun totter down, John, but hand in hand we'll go,—
We'll sleep thegither at the foot, John Anderson, my jo."

There are many things more that might be said, and details which might have been entered into, but I have preferred to set up two or three landmarks in the husband's road of duty. All that I have said I may sum up in this—Husbands love your wives, sympathize with them, confide in them, show that you love them. If any of you are conscious that you have failed in these things, that you have not done your duty to her who put, years ago, her all in your hands, be man enough at once to acknowledge it, at least to yourself; once more let your caresses call back the faded hours of your early love. They will return with a calmer but deeper power. The spring-time may have long passed away, but an autumnal fullness shall linger still around your home.

I cannot close this chapter without expressing what is on my heart about husbands who have christian wives, while they themselves are consciously not Christians. You have sometimes thought that what throws its richest beauty over your wife's life is her piety. You respect and honor it if you are a man. I hope that it is not necessary for me to say much to any reader of these pages about doing nothing to hinder his wife's religion. Of course, you would not do that. For you to put temptations in her way, ask her to go where a disciple of Christ should not, to do things which will dishonor her profession or break the power of her religious principles:—that would be to do a demon's work. But do what you can to help her. Go to church with her, and take some interest in what she holds so dear.

You may be very near your wife, and hold her very fondly to your heart; but, alas, there is a whole world of thoughts and sympathies, of hopes and fears, to which you are all a stranger. Have you never seen your wife pass from her room with wet eyes and come to you silent but with an inexpressible longing in her look? Have you never heard, or thought you did, her voice low in prayer, or caught the sound of sob and a murmured "O God! My husband! Make him Thy child! Let us not be separated forever!" You know well what it meant.

I pray you, let not your wife walk this way alone any more. Give yourself to Jesus Christ. Change those tearful intercessions into praises. Let it not be long before you are able to kneel by her side, and with her give thanks to God that your love will not end with earth, but has something in it of eternity and heaven.

CHAPTER IV.

THE WIFE.

Wives submit yourselves unto your own husbands as unto the Lord.—EPHES. V. 22.

> "By his side there moved a form of beauty,
> Strewing sweet flowers along his path of life,
> And looking up with meek and love-blent duty;
> I called her angel, but he called her wife."

VERY many people read the words of the Scripture which I have placed at the head of this chapter, and others similar to them, with a half-concealed incredulity or a positive rejection. The officiating minister on the marriage-day is charged, half in jest and half in earnest, not to require the bride to "obey," and the laughing wife avers that she did not promise to be obedient to her husband. Everybody knows that just now there is nothing she would not do if the lover-husband bade it; yet the light talk shows a general drift of thought.

The opinion seems to be that these commands were for another age and a different state of society; that they do not belong to our higher civilization.

But, after all, the Bible understands human nature, and the old words have not become obsolete, nor have they ceased to be binding, and that simply because they are founded on the highest philosophy and the first principles of human nature. Indeed, most generally this repudiation of obedience is only a mere matter of imagination, and, though repudiated in word, the obedient spirit has a quiet and deep residence in the wife's heart. If she be a loving and true wife, it surely has. She would not be happy if it were not there.

Reverence, or respect, lies at the foundation of a wife's love for her husband; without it, there can be no true love. No woman can love a man whom she does not respect. It is simply impossible. How often have I heard a young girl, in her true and positive intuition, without thinking that she was expressing any philosophical truth, assert a deep one, as she has exclaimed—" I must be able *to look up* to the man whom I am to love!" or, " I cannot love him, for I do not respect him!" The maiden has never analyzed the feeling, but she has expressed the inner truth.

True affection between husband and wife has its beginnings in this reverence; there may be sentimental preferences, girlish caprices of attachment, but there is nothing that deserves to be called love till she looks up to the man to whom her heart goes out. I am inclined to believe that where love is deepest and truest and most abiding, it is always preceded by such a reverence, a sort of half fear which gives her a tremulous anxiety when in his presence. It may seem groundless to others; it is, perhaps, in reality, very absurd; she may be entirely superior in every respect to the man whom she is beginning to love; but still the reverence, unaccountable as it is, exists, and her love takes its root there. It is a beautiful provision that true affection invests its object with often unpossessed qualities. Love finds what no other eye can, and stands in awe of qualities which no one else imagines.

A husband's eye may be reading this. Here is a point for you of immeasurable importance. If your wife's love had its beginnings in her respect for you, beware that no act of yours shall in the after days do aught to diminish or destroy it! Strive to be what she may only have imagined you; be careful lest you break the hallowed image which she has enshrined in her heart!

On this primal principle, thus lying deep in the mind, I suppose it is that the Bible bases these injunctions and commands of obedience from the wife. They fall in at once with that which makes up a part of her love. This obedience, this reverential subjection, this deferential subordination—it is difficult to get the exact equivalent for the thought—is therefore a part of the wife's duty. It is something absolutely essential to her own happiness in the married life.

For the sake of order and law in the family, there should be a recognized head, and that head should be the natural one. I say natural one, for who does not instinctively require that the husband should be the head? However much we may sometimes talk of the rights of women, after all, no one more than a woman herself is quick to notice, or sure to reprobate, the incongruity of a wife being the head of the house. The sight is not lovely to a woman's eyes. There are few things more unpleasing to women than a family where the wife is supreme and the husband a poor subordinate. She is not admired, and surely the so-called husband evokes no encomiums when he is the subject of their conversation.

When we speak of this obedience which makes a part of the wife's duty, of course the idea of abject, slavish subjection is not in our mind. That has no place in the married life; it can have none where right affection abides. Whenever the hour comes that a husband asserts his authority, or the wife begins to feel it, the hour of a departing love has come. No; as it was at the early dawn of love, so it must be in its high day; the obedient spirit goes hand in hand with love, giving it purity, depth and power, but never a constraint or a chain. The Holy Spirit has Himself given us an illustration which vividly and completely exhibits the true relations of obedience and love—"Husbands love your wives as Christ loved the Church." Then follows the resultant command—the wife must reverence her husband, must yield him an obedience similar to that which the Church gives her Lord—an obedience of love and joy so pure and so free that it is not thought obedience, but is only the willing return of a perpetual affection. This every true wife understands, knows, rejoices, yea glories in. It is her happiness and her pride that she calls a man husband whose power awakens and whose worth compels such feelings. With a true and womanly exultation she delights to do him honor.

Having been met and wooed and won by the man whom she respects, and therefore can love, the wife gives herself to him, and, at the same time, takes into her keeping his honor and his happiness. *She forsakes all others for him.* It is not necessary to linger on what is involved in this—that no other man shall for a moment take her husband's place in her affections. This is too well understood. Whenever another is admired or loved in advance or aside from him, the purity of the soul is gone, and all purity is not far from sacrifice. The wife, and it is no hard duty, is to exalt him as first and above all other men.

But it is to be feared that this matter of forsaking all others for him is not so well understood in all its wide relations. While a dutiful wife sees clearly enough that no other man is for an instant to hold a place in her heart, she may not apprehend so clearly the fact that he is to be supreme there, above associate or friend, above father or mother, sister or brother. She has given them all up for him, and she is to be content with the surrender—must accept what it involves. Her happiness and his greatly depend upon it.

She is to *confide* in him. Her secrets are his secrets; she can have none but what of right belong to him. This may not command the acquiescence of many, yet I am satisfied that they who have thought most deeply and felt most truly on this matter will go with me. There are wives whom all their acquaintances know cannot be trusted to keep anything from their husbands, and they are not made the recipients of a thousand things which it is delightful to tell; but they are not the less honored for that, and they do not fall, in the general estimation, much short of being among the model wives.

But I would speak not so much of concealments as of *revelations*—not of what the wife should not keep from her husband, but rather of what she should not tell of him. "The heart of her husband doth safely trust in her," is a part of that beautiful description of the "virtuous woman whose price is far above rubies," in the 31st chapter of Proverbs; and few things are more important than that he should feel safe in confiding any and all things to her keeping. I have, in another place, spoken at large of the importance of cultivating the feeling of *unity* between husband and wife, and I may here add that the knowledge that he must guard his words and hide his business from his wife goes very far to interrupt and destroy this oneness of spirit.

There are some women who never are at rest while they have anything to tell. The most sacred and inner things of life make no exception to this greed of imparting news: the favored friends, those "very intimate companions, intimate as sisters," are introduced familiarly into the very sanctuary where, it would be supposed, only husband and wife ever walked. These are not, however, very beautiful illustrations of what a wife ought to be.

It cannot be far from the truth to say that not even a sister or a mother ought to stand between a husband and a wife. There are in some, possibly in many a married life, things which weigh upon a wife's heart, and which it would be good if they could be told to these near friends. There may be unkindness or neglect, or worse, that a wife may suffer, and which it is hard to bear alone. The temptation is strong to tell the grievances to those who will give, at least, sympathy in return; and it is hard to resist the temptation. But it must be resisted. When the wife went out from father and mother she forsook them both for her husband, and she must be content with the sacrifice. There are few husbands who do not sometimes give their wives cause for complaint; but that cause ought to be a very serious, even a desperate one, which shall lead a wife to carry it to any one, however dear.

Perhaps difficulties and alienations are produced in this more frequently than in any other way. Little, possibly great things arise in married life, interrupting its even flow, which, were they kept within the precincts of the wife's bosom, might be overcome or removed, but once made known to others become fixed and immovable. The sympathy of a mother or intimate friend may be good, but it has been purchased at a terribly dear price if it be enlisted against a husband. A wife ought to be startled with a thrill of pain and apprehension when she hears a word, even though it be responsive to her own, that derogates from her husband's character. Nothing will sever conjugal affection so rudely and push a husband so far away, as the knowledge that his wife has been complaining of him to another, it matters not who that other is. Whatever the grievance may be, bury it in your own bosom, even though it may make your cheek pale and your form thin. I do not say, indeed, that there may not, that there does not, sometimes come upon a wife from her husband what ought to be told to others; that there may not come a time when she must and can only seek elsewhere the protection and care which she no longer finds from her husband; or when she can abide with him only at a sacrifice of life, or, what is more, of honor. If that evil day has come, surely she may go back to the home whence she came out; she may return to those whom once, confiding in a now faithless husband, she left behind. But short of this, let her pause before she confides the troubles of her married life to another. Unless she sees cause enough for separation or for divorce, let her conceal all within the recesses of her own heart. Time and faithful love may remove the trouble of to-day, and she will smile with joy as she remembers that no stranger eye has ever seen or known that it was there.

But I pass from these things, which are painful even in thought, to speak of some of those minor duties of the wife, upon which, although minor, depend the happiness and even comfort of married life.

The problem of married life, we may say, is—How to retain and strengthen love. *A husband's love must be kept.* When I say this, I am not necessarily implying that it is a thing which is fugitive, or ready to flee away; I am only expressing a common truth of all affection. A mother to keep, must cultivate the love of her child; if she does not she will lose it. The conduct of many a woman leads you to be tolerably certain that she considers her life's grand work to have been all done when she has secured a husband; that when once the irrevocable words have been spoken and the indissoluble bond has been established it is enough; henceforth her husband's love will take care of itself and needs no further care of her's. From almost the marriage-day she begins to neglect all those things by which his heart was first won. It is a great and often, very often, a fatal mistake.

It may be said, as comprehending all, a wife should steadily, and with greater care after her marriage, use all those womanly arts and ways to keep, which her love employed at the first to gain her husband's heart. Too sadly often this is not done.

In those early days of courtship there was a studious endeavor to appear to him in the most pleasing aspect. Nor was there anything either censurable or artful in this; it was the natural, even the beautiful outworking of an affectionate soul. Love desires to appear lovely. Then there was a concealment of all the unamiable traits of character, an exhibition of as many beautiful ones as possible; there was scrupulous care of person and manner, of word and act. It was a natural care prompted at once by respect and perhaps affection. But when courtship is over and the husband safely bound, the whole scene and act changes. Often the poor entrapped man startles at the unexpected discoveries that he makes. He is like a traveller ascending a mountain; he has just been rejoicing in genial breezes and tropical flowers and fruits, but shivers now amid blasted pines and rugged rocks. The wife feels that it is no longer necessary to conceal, but that now she is at liberty to exhibit the less beautiful traits of her character, while she cares little to cultivate and show the lovelier. So the bad comes out and the good retires. It is not at all wonderful now that the love, however strong and deep, which first she secured, should become thin and blasted in this new and wintry air, to which it is so rudely exposed. The love of a true man is one of God's greatest and best gifts. A husband's love is a treasure, and it is worth preserving. Treasures do not keep themselves.

I have just said that the same care should be taken by the wife to retain her husband's heart that was used when it was to be gained; but we may justly go beyond that and assert that even greater pains should be taken in these close intimacies of the married life, when romance has given place to plain and sober reality. Her husband's attachment should grow deeper and deeper as the months go on; the more he learns of his wife, the more should he see to admire and to love. If she be wise and true, such will be the result.

Among the things that a wife should cultivate, is *the Delicacy and Modesty of her early days.* To a high toned man, one of the sweetest attractions is that undefined and indescribable grace which floats like a cloud of beauty round a true woman: that maidenly reserve, yet that transparent frankness; that soul purity which lives and shines in every act and word, and yet does not know and never thinks that it is purity; which can never be put on; which is too ethereal for imitation; which once lost can never be regained; which is as far from prudishness as it is from immodesty; which a bad man hates and cannot understand; which to a good man makes woman like an angel. This need not be lost in the unveiled freedom of wedded intimacy. The wife does indeed give all to her husband; but in that high and holy abandonment, not one grace that made up the pure beauty of her maiden life need be lost. No right minded man would wish it otherwise; he sees and feels its sweet power as fully as ever; nay, it has a deeper hold upon him now, and shines with a calmer, steadier radiance; its magnetic influence reaches out, attracting him to her side, and all the more because the soul of whose beauty he is thus ever catching glimpses, is his alone.

A wife should *cultivate personal attractiveness.* By this I mean every thing which adds to her value as a wife in her husband's eyes. If she would have her husband love her more and more as life advances, she must give him more and more to love. It need hardly be said that she should cultivate moral attractiveness, by her goodness of heart drawing his affections to her. But, what is often not so well understood, she should endeavor to make herself *mentally* attractive. How many a wife complains of the neglect of her husband; that he does not seem to care to be in her society an hour; that he is better pleased to sit with almost any woman than with her; that if he is compelled to be at home an evening with no company but hers, he is silent or restless, and is glad to seek his bed; never once imagining that she herself has any thing to do with these phenomena. If a woman's mind, by her neglect and indolence, has grown barren and dull, so that it is without thoughts that are worthy to be called thoughts; if she be incapable of conversing upon any thing but matters of dress or scandal; if she have no intelligent views of what is going on in the world around her; if she cannot enter into his thoughts or plans; if she present only one long, dreary waste, a vast mental solitude, she ought not greatly to wonder that her husband does not love to walk there, that he is not deeply enamored with her society, or that he sometimes grows bright and cheery when talking with some other woman.

Let the wife cultivate her mind. Marriage ought not to finish learning, if it does school days. She should devote some of her time to this direct end—mental improvement. It is wonderful how much reading, reading, not merely of "ladies' books" and "family" newspapers, with their frequent nonsense and emptiness, but good, useful, solid reading can be accomplished by a very busy housewife and a faithful mother with many little ones around her. I would not have a wife a blue stocking; they are not usually the wives in whom men are very happy. I would not have her a politician, ever ready to tilt a lance with you on questions of statesmanship; but I would have her one whose mind, fairly cultivated, is abreast with the knowledge of the day, and is active enough to meet responsively the approaches of another active and intelligent mind. Were I to descend to particulars, I would say to every wife:—Have a carefully-selected book always at hand, and be in the habit of reading a little from day to day; you need not neglect one duty or fall short of one requirement of your household, and yet at the end of a year you will be astonished at how much you have read; while, in the mental strength and elasticity you have acquired, you will be repaid an hundredfold. Look over the daily newspaper (if you are wide awake, a few minutes will often suffice) so as to know what is going on in the world, and to be able to talk about it intelligently. You will do just as well as, perhaps better than, some male friend who has read it not half so fruitfully, for your husband to compare his thoughts with on the movements of the hour.

Make such efforts at improvement, and you will not long have reason to complain of lonely evenings at home.

Cultivate *physical attractiveness*. I do not know how better to express it. In the days of courtship, every one knows how instinctively careful the maiden is of every thing that bears upon her personal appearance. It is the natural and the beautiful tribute which respect and reverence pay to love. The power of these things is felt without a thought given to the reason of them. The smoothed or braided hair, the pure skin, the well-arranged dress, were attended to with scrupulous exactness; there was a buoyant joyousness in appearing well in the sight of the loved one. There was a power in all this. The maiden instinct was not at fault.

But that power does not fade away when the bridal robes are laid aside. It is just as great now as then. Yet it is not always appreciated so well after marriage as before it. Many a wife laughingly says that "her market is made," and under cover of the jest, which is not all a jest, grows careless of her personal appearance because "it is only her husband" that sees her. It is a mistake. Say what you will, a slovenly wife, in a greasy wrapper, a soiled and rumpled collar, and neglected hair, going slipshod round the house, is not sweetly attractive, she does not call out the same emotions that a different figure would evoke. If a husband comes home to an untidy wife, with the cheek which perhaps he would fain kiss, overhung with elf-locks, it is not greatly surprising that he is not exceedingly demonstrative in his greeting. There is power in these little things, and a wise woman understands them. She knows that there is a difference in the feeling which a man has in meeting a wife in the garb I have sketched, and in coming home to one whose neatness silently but most eloquently tells her husband how much she values his approbation and how highly she respects his love.

Closely connected with this is the duty of *making home attractive.* I mean now simply by keeping the house clean and neat. It need not be elegant, but it can be pleasant. Who of us does not know the difference? You go into one house and you see costly furniture, fair pictures, soft carpets, heavy curtains, yet with them all there is an air of slovenliness and disorder from which you are glad to escape. You go into another; every thing is very plain, even mean, but there is a charm about it, an air of solid comfort or quiet neatness which has a sort of smile of welcome. This last is attainable in the humblest home.

There are few men, however terrible they may be to notable housekeepers in upsetting and misplacing things, who do not love cleanliness and order in their home. I verily believe that many a man has been driven away from his home by the demon of untidiness. There is something which strikes a man with a chill of discouragement, to come at night to a home which is in perpetual disorder, to uncleanliness, to the noisy bustle of "getting things to rights," and the nameless horrors of fruitless attempts at house-keeping. I would say to every wife:—See that your house, however plain it may be, is a clean and orderly one; greet your husband in neat garb and welcome him at least to a well swept and settled room; entertain him at a table, which, though it may not have a sumptuous supper upon it, yet is always covered with white cloth and plates that will reflect back the smile of your welcome. Should your house be one of elegance, remember that poor house-keeping will deprive both furniture and pictures and plate of all their value to a husband that loves his home. To sum it all up:—throw around your home such an air of coziness and comfort that neither club-room nor lounging-place shall have any chance in the comparison; that your husband shall be compelled to think it the cheeriest spot in all the world.

These outward things, however, are not all, or even the most important in giving to a husband an attractive home; there must be the perpetual *sunshine of pleasant looks and words.* The repeated and vivid comparisons of the Wise Man in the book of Proverbs about the contentious woman and the continual dropping on a very rainy day, have a terrible significance to some men. No one loves to be met on his entrance at night-fall, with sour looks and upbraiding speeches; nor to bear during a winter's evening the bombardment of sharp or sarcastic words dropped like hot shot between the paragraphs of his daily paper. Nor should the wife who gives such things think it marvellous if her husband often has occasion to "meet a friend," or "attend a committee meeting," when supper-time has passed.

On the other hand, he must be a bad man upon whom smiles and words of affectionate greeting when he enters home have no tender and softening influence. I do not say that it is always possible for a wife after a weary day of annoyance, fatigue and anxiety with household duties, to put on an air of unmingled sweetness and cheerfulness. I know that some men expect that, and I know that in expecting it they are unreasonable. I hope that in the previous chapter, when speaking of the husband's duties, I referred sufficiently to the point. Yet even though she cannot always seem perfectly cheerful and smiling, she can avoid pouring out a stream of fretfulness and fault-finding, the pent-up volume of her annoyances, upon him; she need not make his coming the occasion of opening the valve which shrilly pierces the ear with its blast. A good husband will, as I have said before, sympathize with his wife's cares, and lighten them with appreciative words, but she should be careful not to make them the only, or the main topic of her conversation with him. If it is at all possible, she should *show contentment and satisfaction.* It is hard for a man who has honestly labored to provide for his family, and, with all the skill he posseses, has endeavored to make them happy, to find only repining and fault-finding as his reward; and he must be a man of unbounded good nature, or of iron will, who does not become discouraged and give over efforts which clearly are so fruitless. If, on the contrary, a husband finds that his well-intended attempts are noticed and appreciated, that they call out kind expressions of approbation and affectionate thanks, it will not be long before he becomes enthusiastic in his plannings, even were there no other motive before him than the sunny smile and the glad words of surprise that he knows are sure to meet him at his home. Oh, there is power in a wife's smiles; they are like the summer sunshine and the dew; they glow and they distill gently, but they call out whole harvests of teeming good.

Among these minor but mighty things, let me mention *little and delicate attentions.* Perhaps you will know at once what I mean. There are many wives who love their husbands with a devoted love, who would sacrifice their life without hesitation to save his, who in times of sickness or danger are all devotion, but who yet on ordinary occasions never give an outward sign of tenderness or affection. It may be a sufficient explanation for some that it is not their nature; but it seems to me that such a nature should be cultivated into one of a better kind. Our life is made up both in its pleasures and its troubles of little things, and the man or woman who does not recognize the fact, will make a great many failures, and miss a great many joys. A glance of the eye, a touch of the hand, has in it at times, a magnetic power which not every one knows how to measure. Let a wife use that power. I know that there are women who never find time to sit quietly by their husband's side; who would consider it an immense waste to be there without a bit of sewing in hand; who would consider it very foolish to be kissed by their husbands, who would absolutely smile at the absurdity of her head upon his shoulder; these things belonged possibly to some far back and girlish days, but like other childish things have long since been put away. But still there are those who know differently; they ask and they give what is better than jewels.

These little attentions—a hand laid on his

shoulder as some wives know how, half thoughtlessly, an arm slipped quietly within his as she stands by his side, will give a gentle thrill of satisfaction which cannot be expressed; they are better than mere words, have a deeper tone in them, and are more full of music. There need not be perpetual fondling, especially before others, but these little things, like bubbling fountains by the way-side, are recognized as at once the effect and the evidence of love which by reason of its own fullness must have an outlet.

A wife should be *careful of her husband's interests.* She should know and enter sufficiently into his business to understand what expenditures of their means—I will not say his—are right and proper. Too sadly often a husband has been ruined by his wife's thoughtless extravagance, which while he saw and feared it, he either could not or would not check. She had neither taste nor heart to know anything about business; she did not and could not know what the money cost of labor, how it was gotten, or how much of it there was; she has gone into expenditures and urged her husband into them, while his affection for her and his pride in her have helped on the evil work, till disaster and even ruin have been the result. Yet this wife, responsible as she is, had she known her work, rather than do it, would have cut off her right hand.

Let a wife practice the care and attention to her husband's interests that daily show him that she has these interests at heart, that she is neither selfish nor thoughtless, and she will not feel the want of anything her husband's means can give her.

A wife should *defend and hold to her husband, even when all else and all others have failed him.* There is a sublimity in the self-sacrifice of a wife that clings to the side of her husband, though he lies, like a shipwrecked bark, on life's tempest-swept strand. I have seen a wife watching with unwearied care over an imbruted man whom rum had made a beast; and when all others could no longer abide him, when all others had given him over in hopeless abandonment, still lingering near, a guardian spirit hovering over a lost soul; and I have thought it the exquisite, the supremest proof of a wife's devotion. Here was faithfulness that lived while all but the name of husband had gone; honor which would not die even though all that could be honored had gone into corruption. It was woman-like; and I think it will have its reward.

I wish to say a few words before I close this chapter, to those wives who, while they are *professors of religion themselves, have husbands who are not.* To such let me say, with all the emphasis that I am capable of using:—Exert your Christian influence steadily and without compromise. Many a wife has made a fatal mistake here. She has honestly been of the opinion that she could have the best influence over her husband by yielding her religious feelings and habits to his. So she has joined him, for example, in visiting places of amusement, which otherwise she would have avoided; she has sanctioned, if not encouraged him in practices and associations which, in her heart, she could not approve, and this because she has feared to alienate his affections. The result has been that, instead of winning him, she has lost him. She has not brought him to sympathize with her religious feelings, because she has never shown any; she has held them out of sight, and they have had no power over him, and could have none. She has lost much of her own religion, which could hardly live in such a stifling atmosphere, and she has committed him to the full sweep of all the unhallowed forces exerted upon him. In many an instance he has become estranged, perhaps unfaithful, from the subtile influence of a dead religion in his wife, and because that which alone could have held him back was withdrawn.

Do not, christian wife, fall into this error. Do not lay aside your religion because your husband is not with you in it. Maintain scrupulously your habits of reading the Bible and of secret prayer; attend regularly and punctually upon your church; be a consistent Christian in everything; do nothing which is not in strict accordance with your christian principles; show your husband what a christian wife is. You will surely meet a blessed reward. You may gain him for Christ if you do; you, more than all others, may keep him away from Christ if you do not.

Oh, the power of a good wife! God's best earthly gift to man! What lines of care can she smooth out of furrowed brows! What sunshine can she pour in upon clouded hours! What ramparts of defence can she put up in hours of temptation! What prayers are more mighty than those that gush from her heart! You may walk, if you will, an angel by his side, and, it may be, heaven will be more complete because you did.

CHAPTER V.

PARENTS.

Train up a child in the way he should go, and when he is old he will not depart from it.—PROVERBS xxii. 6.

It is no little thing when a fresh soul
And a fresh heart, with their unmeasured scope
For good, not gravitating earthward yet,
But circling into diviner periods,
Are sent into this world. LOWELL.

WITHIN the limits which I have set for myself, and in a single chapter, to attempt any detail of rules for family training, would be useless. I shall intentionally pass by some topics naturally presenting themselves to one in contact with the subject, that I may linger on others less obvious but of equal importance.

The responsibility of a parent is so often talked about that we are in danger of losing, by reason of the triteness of the word, the seriousness of the fact. None of us have ever risen to a full appreciation of it; none of us can reach it unless we be able to explore all the hidden avenues by which one soul approaches another, or look over the eternal tract of a soul's history, and follow the connected chain of causes which make it what it is and what it will be. This, however, we may say—to be a parent is to be the occasion of the entrance of an intelligent being on an endless life, a life which shall, in one of two worlds, be filled with unspeakable joys or immeasurable sorrows; it is to stand at the origin of a life and to start it on an eternal career; it is to be placed at the beginning of this great existence with a signet in your hand which you shall, in spite of yourself, stamp upon an immortal soul, the impression to last through its whole history; it is to have a new and intense meaning given to every word and look and thought of yours, since thought and look and word perpetuate themselves in the being whose destiny is linked with yours forever.

It is said that, in a certain gallery of paintings, are two pictures hanging side by side. The one is that of a boy at his mother's knee, with the angel smile of happy childhood upon a face of passing purity and sweetness; the other is that of a prisoner in his cell, a man prematurely old, with grizzly locks and beard, an eye fierce and wicked, and from every feature the hardened villain glaring out. You look upon the one and are entranced with its heavenly beauty, and you instinctively shrink from the sinister look of the other. You are struck with the strange contrast, but have a deeper interest awakened when you are told that they are life portraits, and of the same person; the angel-like child and the demon-like man are one! The difference is vast between them, but the gulf has very often been passed in this sinful world. How shall the father, as he stands meditatingly beside the cradle of his boy, tell through what scenes of virtue or of crime he shall go? How shall the mother tell whether or not the sweet baby-girl in her arms shall die, a lonely and forsaken outcast, in some garret on a winter's night?

Such thoughts as these have a sort of truthfulness in them, and yet they are not all true. The coming history of a child is uncertain, only when contemplated as a future unrelated to present influences. The baby child may one day become a murderer; the two pictures may be life-like, but whether they shall be, will depend on what has been done to shape the soul that beamed in the infant face or scowled in the man's. Tell what influences will, all along, be exerted upon that child, beginning here in these cradle-days and continued through childhood, and you shall not be wholly uncertain what he will be; know them, and you may cast the horoscope of his future, and still be neither astrologer nor prophet.

The Author of this universe has connected causes and effects, and they are more or less constant and invariable. They exist as fully in the moral world as in the physical, and they are, if possible, more constant, invariable, and more to be relied upon in the former than in the latter. If you thrust your arm into the fire, you expect to be burned; if you throw a heavy body from a height, you expect it to fall. The forces of heat and gravitation prevail according to their regulating laws. So in the great world of right and wrong, good influences tend to good results. The result may, indeed, be prevented by creature will, which brings in an antagonistic power, but the law is—good produces good.

I believe that God has made this especially true in the sphere of parental influence. Here the laws of cause and effect are found to be marked and palpable. If there were no observation and experience to teach us, the words of the Scripture are sufficient: "Train up a child in the way he should go, and when he is old he will not depart from it." The language is very plain and emphatic. Here is cause and effect; right parental training will not only produce good results in the life of the child, but these results will be *permanent*, the child shall not only walk in the right way, but no future influences shall be strong enough to turn him away from it.

There is a profound significance in the words by which that remarkable interview between the Jehovah Angel and Abraham, recorded in Genesis (xviii. 17-20), is introduced: "And the Lord, said, Shall I hide from Abraham that thing which I do? seeing that Abraham shall surely become a great and mighty nation, and all the nations of the earth shall be blessed in him? *For I know him that he will command his children and his household after him, and they shall keep the way of the Lord* to do justice and judgment; that the Lord may bring upon Abraham that which he hath spoken of him." The great and prosperous future was known because the parental influence was certain to be beneficent. Oh, what a motive and encouragement is here for parental faithfulness! What an indication of a parent's power! Here he stands and shapes the future of his child; he need not fear that this training of his shall be either fruitless or evanescent; it shall last and it shall be prevalent over all other powers. What, I may add, what a direful import do the words have when you contemplate the life of a wicked man! Why was it wicked? What were the powers which brought about this baleful product? Why were the right influences absent? Why was not the training given to hold him in the path of right?

I have thought of this matter much and long, and have observed as I have been able, and the longer I live, and the more I see, the more I am convinced of both the truth of this Scripture and the responsibility of parents for the future charac- of their children. I believe in the perfect freedom of every human being, whether child or man; but so well convinced am I of the prevalence of the great laws of cause and effect in the family, that I believe that we are not only warranted, but compelled to look, and we do instinctively look back to parental influence, whenever we see either a good or an evil life. Is it too much to say, that however you may at first question it, you have never known a bad man, the evil of whose life you cannot more or less closely connect with wrong or defective training in early life? If he had been rightly trained he would have walked in the way he should go; he would not have departed from it.

When I look at the measureless power given to the parent, when I look at all that depends on his right action, I cannot believe that this matter of child-training is uncertain; and when I look at the Bible and attentively consider all that God has written there about it, I am sure that it is not. Let a parent take the word of God, study it well, let him believe that its wisdom is greater than his own, and so trust it; act as it tells him to act; let him on bended knee and with docile soul inquire what is God's will and his own duty;

let him ask wisdom and—it is one of the things that we are authorized to be confident of—he shall be guided, and he shall not be disappointed at the results.

But, alas, the difficulty is we do not believe, as we ought, God's word, our faith is too feeble, and we are too indolent and too self-willed to follow its teachings. Parents do not pray enough over their child-training. It would not be wonderful at all if some father and some mother should be reading this, who have never yet uttered one heartfelt and earnest prayer that *God would help* them train their children. Do you wonder that you are unsuccessful? I do not. When, with a heart-sick feeling of your own ignorance and weakness, you bow with tears before God, asking His help and His blessing, you will do it better than you do it now.

Here, then, upon these principles, I would base my first remark: *Let every parent endeavor to have a full and clear appreciation of his position and influence upon his child.* It will be in the future what you, the father and the mother, make it. You may seek to evade the responsibility by incredulity; you may believe these views to be all wrong, but it will still be true that God has put you where you cannot but influence your children; and whether you act or do not act, you shall mould their life. You are shut up to training them right. You cannot be negative here. Not to train at all is to train badly and wickedly. It is for you, with all these interests at stake, to know how to do your work well. You will, at all events, do a work upon your children; you are doing it day by day. The simple question is, what shall be its character? Shall it go to make a good and useful man, or shall its product be a harmful and wicked one? It is only a question of results; they will follow what you are doing now; you, on your responsibility, are to declare what they shall be.

A true appreciation of parental power and position will go far toward a right performance of parental duty, and in presenting it I have presented what may be the key to much of family training. There are some points, however, which are, perhaps, not thought of by parents as much as they should be; among them let me mention—

Sympathy with Childhood. It is very easy for a parent to err here; and, perhaps, all the more, because the sense of responsibility is great. Under it parents are liable to assume a distant and unsympathetic attitude toward their children, and to give them, unconsciously, the idea that they are out of the circle of a child's thoughts and feelings. This is unfortunate, for it deprives a parent of much of his power. You can do no one much good if he thinks you do not understand him, nor enter into his feelings; and none are so quick as children to detect and measure the inner attitude of any one toward them. There are some persons who, do what they will, strive hard as they may, can never be favorites with children; and there are others who, seemingly without an effort, attract them to their side; simply, I suppose, because the one has what the other has not, a natural sympathy with childhood; and the quick intuition of the child feels it. This sympathy is not, therefore, a mere matter of will; some have it by nature and some are with out it. But it can be cultivated.

Fathers, it seems to me, are more in danger of coming short here than mothers. They are less with their children, and this, were there no other reason, tends to remove them somewhat away from the child's world, while the trains of daily thought all favor the tendency. So it often happens that the father, returning from business cares, does not readily walk in the paths that have been trod all day by the little ones at home. Their noise and their questions trouble him, and they easily understand that the hour which hastens them off to bed is very welcome to him. Parents should make this sympathy with their children a direct object of attainment. They should never forget that they were once children themselves, and it will be of immense service to remember *just how they felt and thought when they were little boys and girls.* If these by-gone days were more kept in mind, children would be saved hours of fruitless longing and tears of bitter disappointment which ought never to oppress their hearts or mark their cheeks.

There is something wrong when children do not care to be where their parents are, or do not feel free at their play when father or mother is by, and it ought to awaken thoughtfulness when a parent finds that his presence is to them no welcome thing. On the other hand, I know of few more pleasant sights or sounds than the glad shout of welcome which greets a father as his children catch a glimpse of his form in the distance, and the merry race for the prize of his hand to hold as he comes to his door. You need not be told that here is one who is not far from the circle in which his children move. It does not injure a father now and then to take a turn with his boys at marbles or at bat and ball, or for a mother to give careful attention to the toilet of a doll; indeed, these are the things which keep up the freshness of his own spirit and rob the years of their power to make him old; and what is of greater importance in the eyes of children, they keep hanging on the boughs of advancing years the full foliage of pleasant summer days; it does not appear so sad a thing to grow old; at least they know that manhood does not lose its hold upon the child. It is this recognized sympathy which draws a child to his parent. This leads me to another topic—

Parents should bind their children lovingly to them. I know that this will seem a very trite remark. But I am, too, well aware that while every father and mother wishes to secure the love of their children, there are multitudes who entirely fail in doing it. Their children when young prefer to be with them, rather because they are accustomed to their society than from any deep-seated affection, but as soon as they are old enough to seek other companionships and associations, those of father and mother are gladly forsaken. The parent has no hold on the child, and filial love has a very shadowy existence, if it exist at all. After every allowance has been made for the waywardness of children, one would not be far astray were he to assert that when a parent has failed to secure the warm love of his child, it is usually the parent's own fault. Filial love is natural; children are born to love their parents; the germs of the tree are there, and if it never grows, or only dies, when it is just above the ground, it is because no culture has kept it alive.

Parents must cultivate the affection of their children with greater care than they cultivate their minds. The love of your child is of no such nature that it will stay by you if you do not try to keep it. The heart of your child is to you of more importance than his intellect, and it will not add to your happiness, if while you have made the one brilliant, you have turned the other away from you. Here in the deep-toned love of your child is a jewel of priceless value to him and to you; you can afford to give care and labor to keep it safely.

With this end in view—*Teach your children to confide in you.* In whom should a child confide if not in a mother or a father? They would seem the natural resort in any time of perplexity. Yet who does not know that the sons and daughters who unbosom themselves to father and mother are exceptional children? The most seek their confidants every where rather than at home. It is worthy of consideration by every parent whether this is necessary—whether any thing in their conduct toward their children has tended to produce it. If from the first the sympathy, of which I have spoken, has been cultivated, and through the early years of childhood the boys or girls have grown up with the idea that father and mother understand all about them, and take the deepest interest in their affairs, those concealments which are so often sorrowful to the parent and dangerous to the child, would not be so frequent.

Children should be able to feel that they are certain to find a sympathetic friend in father or mother. We should beware therefore of making light of any thing that our children consider important. We should put ourselves while they are young on the plane of their thoughts and feelings, be at pains to exhibit our interest, and so encourage them to tell their little troubles to us. Then in the after years, when they are called to confront matters on which perhaps hang their life's happiness, we shall not be strangers to them; and we shall be able to help them with counsel such as a parent alone can give. A doll's dress torn, a kite stick broken may tell on a long future.

Especially should a parent be lovingly watchful of that delicate and critical time when the child passes out of youth into manhood or womanhood. All the old associations of childhood are with you as an almost present reality; with your son and daughter they are things of the past. *You must not too long think of them as children.* Gently, gracefully, naturally as you can, lift them to the level of your man and woman thought and feeling. Walk with them arm in arm, talk with them as if you had forgotten that they were lately children, consult them as if you had confidence in them and their judgment; let the silken cords of parental authority which childhood felt, transform themselves into ornaments of grace and beauty which you hang about their neck. So the instinctive love of a boy and girl shall imperceptibly change to the intelligent and undying devotion of a man and woman. You may have lost childhood with the inevitable flight of years, but you have gained manhood forever.

It should be the aim and endeavor of every parent *to make home as attractive as possible to their children.* There is such a thing as throwing round a home so many beautiful things—I mean not beautiful in art to catch the eye, but beautiful in thought and association, holding the heart—that children shall cling to it with an undying love. The point which we have before us, is that of binding our children to us; and I believe that here, in making homes pleasant, is an instrumentality whose importance is not understood as it ought to be. The complaint is often made by parents, and with sadly too frequent truthfulness, that as soon as their children become old enough to mingle in society their home is forsaken, they seem uneasy and restless when compelled to remain even for a single evening there, and almost any other place seems to be preferred to that where father and mother and brothers and sisters are found. This complaint is made with a tone of deep regret, but at the same time perhaps the parents who make it have no suspicion that, after all, the cause of what they deprecate is found in themselves. No child, however sentimental, will love a home simply because it has the name of one. If we would have our children love it, we must make it lovely—we must give them something to love in the home.

Now if the principle ideas which a child has of his home are, that it is a place where he gets his meals and where he sleeps; where, if he is little, he is perpetually found fault with; where he must keep quiet; where at night-fall he must sit stupidly waiting till bed-time; or, if he have grown older, he can only deem it a dreary room in which he must employ himself as best he may, while the father sits at his paper or dozes in his chair, and the mother is silently busy with her sewing or her book; if such be the aspect of home, one need not wonder that children learn to look elsewhere for pleasure, and seek to find amusement in other circles, or that home is forsaken as soon as it is possible to leave it.

It is practicable to make a home so delightful that children shall have no disposition to wander from it or prefer any other place; it is possible to make it so attractive that it shall not only firmly hold its own loved ones, but shall draw others into its cheerful circle. Let the house, all day long, be the scene of pleasant looks, pleasant words, kind and affectionate acts; let the table be the happy meeting-place of a merry group, and not a dull board where a silent, if not sullen company of animals come to feed; let the meal be the time when a cheerful laugh is heard and good things are said; let the sitting-room, at evening, be the place where a smiling company settle themselves to books or games till the round of good-night kisses are in order; let there be some music in the household, music not kept like silk and satins to show to company, but music in which father and mother and sister and brother join; let young companions be welcomed and made for the time a part of the group, so that daughters shall not deem it necessary to seek the obscurity of back parlors with intimate friends, or to drive father and mother to distant apartments; in a word, let the home be surrounded by an air of cozy and cheerful good-will; then children need not be exhorted to love it, you will not be able to tempt them away from it.

The ties which bind a child to home are created not so much out of great as from little things; some of them I have hinted at, and many more will suggest themselves to a wise parent. There should be a good many holidays in the home. I believe in anniversaries, and I love, by observing them, to connect time with events, and so give to both a deeper interest. The birth-days of a family should be always noticed, and, in someway, celebrated. The busy preparation of the whole household to make some present to father or mother or sister or brother on a birth-day or holiday; the many plannings, the working in by-corners and at odd times; the bundling of work out of sight as the step of the favored one is heard; the careful stowing of gifts away till the appointed time; and then, when the looked-for day has come, the presentations, the confused and merry voices, the filled eye, the choked voice, the heart too full to speak in words, memory touched as with an angel's hand, love that can only look its thanks—all these! who can tell their sweet and mighty power? A home familiar to such scenes, will it, can it be one that children shall not love? No, no, from it, when the inexorable time comes to go away, daughters shall pass with sobs of sorrow, and sons with pressed lips and swimming eyes, and while mother lives it will be home still, home, though years have gone and other homes have claimed them.

When you have made such a home for your children, you have thrown around them a hallowed influence which time and distance and temptation cannot sever—an influence for good that shall be simply unmeasured

Few, comparatively, appreciate the immense moral power of that which meets the eye of a child in his home. Order and neatness, which surround him like an atmosphere; forms of beauty which attract him; are not simply pleasing in themselves, but are perpetually reaching out, and, by touching the soul itself, forming the disposition and the heart.

I have known a father select a picture, only a lithograph, inexpensive, but chosen from among many because of the sweet face of a little girl who looks up at you, with needle in her fingers, from her work, while a gentle smile is lighting up every feature; and place it in his dining-room with the sole purpose that the ever-beaming countenance should exert its influence over the little ones of the household. Who can say that no gathering cloud of anger or discontent has been chased away by that sunny look! No one can measure the quiet influence of things like that.

In these days, when through the lithograph and the chromo treasures of art are within the reach of almost every one, it is not difficult to adorn a very humble home with what will be an ever-present and ever-exerted power for good. Pictures and statuettes should be chosen, not alone for their beauty, but chiefly for their influence on the family; to deepen the purity, elevate the character and strengthen the moral life of all who look upon them. We should educate our children morally through the random glances of their eye.

The element of beauty is, one is almost tempted to believe, native to every child, and can be made a force in the soul. I am not able to name the author of the following; I have found it as a floating waif, but I adopt the language and endorse its admirable teaching: "In the religious nurture of children we should address ourselves, far more than we do, to the sentiment of beauty in their minds. We are eager to fill our homes with beautiful and costly objects, but are slow to fill our minds and theirs with beautiful thoughts. We are impatient to clothe ourselves and them in the finest apparel, but are altogether too patient of repulsive habits and deforming dispositions. We want to see, and make them see, that beauty, taste and elegance are great things; and that all meanness, ill-temper, fretfulness, falsehood and wrong are utterly ugly. We need to see for ourselves and help them to feel the unspeakable attractiveness of moral beauty; the loveliness of truth, the charm of a sweet forgiving spirit, and the splendor of self-sacrifice; that every bad habit is a sin against taste and beauty, as well as an offense against the Holy Ghost."

There is enough said about the education of the intellect and of the morals, but possibly enough is not said of the education of the heart.

The one is as capable of cultivation as the other. A child, naturally of an impassive, unaffectionate temperament, introduced into a family where love abounds and is manifested, where the different members are accustomed to exhibit it in the numberless and nameless acts which make such a family beautiful, cannot, after a while, but do the same things; the most frigid nature must thaw under a sky so genial The converse is just as true. I have seen a child, natively most tender and susceptible, a boy with a heart all affection, and feelings like æolian strings, ready to vibrate at every breath, grow up a cold-hearted, undemonstrative man; just because he had lived under an unfortunate and mistaken family influence, in which no effort had been made to give play to the movements of his deeper and gentler nature, and where all was calculated to suppress and stifle them. Without vice, yet with many of the finer and tenderer characteristics gone, one would well wonder how such a little child could have become such a man. I, looking back over all the training, have no difficulty in accounting for it.

Perhaps some one will say—We do not wish

our children, and especially our boys, to be of so soft a nature that they shall feel deeply everything which touches their sensibilities; we wish them to be men. In reply to such a parent, argument would be of not much account. If an affectionate disposition, the beautiful and nobler sensibilities of the soul seem to him of no value, but rather to be eradicated, nothing can be said. But to a parent who sees a beauty and a priceless value in a sympathetic heart, to whom manifested love is very precious, to such a parent, I would say:—Give care to your childrens' affections. When your little one would throw his arms around your neck and imprint kisses on your cheek, do not push him away for fear he will rumple your smooth linen or disarrange your hair. When, in your hurry, he would detain you, or even call you back for a "good-bye kiss," or bring you to his crib for one more "good-night," do not consider it too much trouble, or permit him to see that you think it so. Make much of it, for believe me, in the end, it is much. You may, by only welcoming these natural outgoings of childhood's heart, make a summer of delight to you; like little birds, that will only fly away to return no more if you are rude, they will come and nestle in your bosom, and sing you many a song that shall be as the whisperings of angels.

There is just here one mistake that I would guard you against. It is this:—The idea that you can best secure the affection of your children by allowing them to be disobedient. No error could be more fatal. A parent never yet held the love of his children by any such process; and thousands have lost it forever. If you wish your child to grow up with no love for you, and little for any one else, let him have his own way. If you excuse his faults, instead of condemning them; if you shield him from punishment because you do not care to see him suffer, you will not be disappointed. He will abundantly reward you by and by, as he will thrust you behind his back without a thought. If the future brings to you some bitter experience of the utter heartlessness of your child; if your very heart dies to see how little he cares for you, remember that it was because you would be a wicked parent, and would permit your child to be disobedient. I will not stop to explain how obedience makes love and joy, I will only ask you to look at the families where obedience is the law; you shall see a household full of love, where the very footfall of father or mother makes every one astir with gladness.

There is one other suggestion which I make for the training of children; it may be stated comprehensively—*Train your children for usefulness and for independence.* The topic is wide-reaching, and I can but hint at a few points. In the material world there are a great many things which are made only for ornament, and they fulfill their end when they have given pleasure to the eye. It is not so in the social world. No man or woman is simply ornamental. Many, no doubt, think themselves so, but they are mistaken. If they are not positively useful, they are excrescences. Every child should be trained with the full purpose of accomplishing something for the good of the world. This observation has force, I apprehend, more in respect to the girls of a family than the boys. On every side you will see daughters trained in such a way that if they are ever fit for any thing, when they become women, it will be because they learn it after they have gone out from their mother's home. A girl with little or no musical ability is kept for years wasting, daily, precious hours over an afflicted instrument to make an indifferent performer, to whom polite people listen with sufferance; she is made to daub a few pieces of canvas with many a helping touch from her teacher; with vast labor taught to murder some French phrases, and what, perhaps, will give you a smile, is able to say that she has studied Latin; in the meanwile, enlargement or furniture of mind seems not to be thought of; history, science, literature are unknown, intelligent conversation is impossible, and household knowledge not to be mentioned.

Such girls are apt to have mothers who make themselves household drudges, waiting-maids for their daughters; mothers who spend much of their time in the kitchen or sitting-room with work-basket in lap, while daughters are simpering in the parlor or chatting gaily in the street. The fault is not with the poor girls; you may not admire them, but you should not hastily blame them. Many of them are really girls of native good sense and force of character. When they become old enough, they will regret and mourn over the training they have had; and under very many disadvantages will set about remedying its defects; but at present you should put the responsibility and the blame where it belongs—on a weak, and perhaps it would not be too harsh to say, wicked mother. A mother has no right to train a daughter so that she shall be wholly unfitted for any true life-work. Mothers, train your daughters so that they shall be women, women worth the name.

Much is often said by some people of the necessity of a certain kind of accomplishments, so called, to make sons and daughters gentlemen and ladies. The dancing master is sent for, and the children are put through all the niceties of that distinguished and dignified business—to give them, forsooth, grace! to make them polite! I have heard of the process and seen the results, and I cannot say that they were greatly pleasing. I have seen pupils long under the instruction, with hardly the first elements of grace or any thing which could give them any true title to the character of polite people. No, a true gentleman or lady was never yet created by the dancing-master; the origin is back of that. It must be born in the parent or in the child, or be the product of a new birth of soul. It is a very sad and humiliating confession, that parents have to send for a teacher of steps to show a child how to be graceful and polite.

Grace and true gentility are the fruit of family life. Children will be abroad what they are at home. If parents would have them truly polite men and women abroad, let there be a reign of true politeness in the family. If children see a daily example of refined attentions between father and mother, they will catch the spirit and the form of them, they know not how; if habits at the table, in the parlor, in the nursery are guarded and formed aright, all will take care of itself, when they are away from home. I know, indeed, that some people are born with a grace and courtliness of manner which will manifest themselves in the face of almost bad surroundings; but I know, too, that vulgarity and indecorum at home never yet gave birth to delicacy and refinement abroad. The outside will declare the inner life. Let good manners be the rule of the family, and you need have no fear that your children will not be both easy and decorous wherever they may be placed.

And for this there is nothing so potent as true family religion. Christianity makes gentlemen. He who is in the habitual exercise of the benevolent, self-sacrificing, kind and gentle characteristics of a christian, will be a well-bred man. So in the family, where the spirit of true religion has a home, there will be a perpetual influence to refine, soften and elevate every member of it.

Childhood is not long; it is very short. How very brief, indeed, it is! Some twelve years or so cover it all. While you are scarcely aware, your little babe has become a boy, and while you have only become accustomed to thinking him a child, he has passed out of childhood forever. What parent has not had it come home to him with a deep tinge of melancholy?

There is but one childhood for your little ones. Oh, then, make it for them all that you can. Make it completely good, redolently sweet in the present, radiant in the past. It is a mournful thing to give them an unhappy childhood. Sad, sad, indeed, is it for one to look back on a childhood which has little in it that he cares to think of. Fill it now with things which will be good by and by to hold in memory. Perhaps all that your children will remember of you will be connected with their childhood; perhaps ere it has gone, mother and father will be away, living only in recollection. Make that memory hallowed and sweet.

Now is your time. Lose not your children's childhood. Lose not your boys and girls. They will not be such long. Make the most of them. Then, if God shall permit you to look upon them, men and women, they will cling to you as in the bygone days, when they stood by your knee or nestled in your arms. You will be mother and father, they will be children still. If while they are young, they die, it will be blessed for you to think that the brief years that God left them with you, you made as bright and as happy as you could; if you leave them at God's call, they will think of you fondly with smiles of love and gratitude shining through every tear of sorrow that falls.

The right training of a family of children is a work as difficult as it is monotonous; yet I am of the opinion, that the chief thing is for a parent to be clearly impressed with its greatness, and to be really in earnest. An honest desire, common sense, and above all a sincere looking to God, will enable any parent to accomplish a work for their children which will make them a glory and a blessing. I say, a sincere looking to God. I do not know how others may feel, but it seems to me that a parent who has never felt the need of a higher wisdom than his own, and better help than man's, has yet caught scarcely a glimpse of what it is to be a parent. I know that he has never yet understood what it is to train a child for eternity.

Father! Mother! can it be that this child of yours shall in the relentless future be what you are now making it? Can it be that you are standing at the beginnings of an existence which shall be greatly what you to-day are shaping and you never pray! Never ask God to help you be a good father, a good mother! Alas, alas, for you and for your child!

You look upon your children with pride and delight; you sometimes bend over them sleeping till the mists hide them from your eyes; you long with an unutterable desire that their future life should be happy; you would give your own to make it certain; you wish, sometimes you think of it, you wish that they one day may be in heaven. What, I ask you, are you doing to make it sure?

You have them, (I know that some of you without a hope in Christ do,) you have them bow at your knee in prayer, but you yourselves never truly pray for them! How can you, when your own hearts are withheld from God? More than you think, they look and they wonder at you. Perhaps they will fail of heaven because you never took them to Jesus. How could you, when you have never gone yourself?

By all the love which your heart has for them, I ask you as you lay this book aside, to seek some secret place, and in an agony of supplication give yourself to your Saviour. The consecration may have in it eternal life for your children.

CHAPTER VI.

CHILDREN.

Honor thy father and thy mother as the Lord thy God hath commanded thee; that thy days may be prolonged and that it may go well with thee, in the land which the Lord thy God giveth thee.—DEUT. v. 16.

Pure as the unsullied streams that flow
  From rocky founts through vales below;
Holy as angel's thoughts above,
  Is that blest one—a mother's love.

ANON.

To you your father should be as a god.—SHAKSPEARE.

I DO not intend in this chapter to address simply the very young, but rather all those who have parents yet remaining to them. The great and beautiful obligations of filial duty do not end with childhood, they abide in increasing power as long as a parent lives to bless or be blessed.

Instead of being diminished by the lapse of years, they but grow and deepen in the consciousness of a right hearted child, as the years advance and he becomes more capable of understanding what is it to have a father or a mother.

Next to the great commands which have reference to God, there are none given with such emphasis and accompanied with such clear and positive promises as those of which the scripture which heads this chapter is an example. The commandment of which this is a repetition has a peculiar place in the decalogue. It is the fifth commandment not by accident but by design. It is, so to speak, the transition command between the first and the second tables of the law. The first four precepts relate to our duty to God, the last five to our duty to man; this stands midway between them, to show that the duties which a child owes to his parents are the next lower and only lower to those which he owes to God; while they rise above and stand before all that he owes to other men.

The parent during all the first years of a child's life stands to him in the place of God. The parental law is all that he can understand,

and he is to obey it implicitly, as by-and-by he shall be called upon to obey God's law. This parental law is therefore rudimentary to the divine, and is in the Ten Commandments made a part of it. So it stands in this middle place among them, lower than the obligations due to God, the highest of those due to men. So important is it deemed to the well being of man and so pleasing is it to God, that there are promises attached to it as to no other of the commandments. The peculiarity of the promises, too, is striking—they are promises of present and earthly good; long life and prosperity are the rewards held out to the child that honors father and mother.

One of the saddest evidences of the depravity of the race is that the world is full of disobedient and ungrateful children. There are indeed times when to the best, the *duty* of filial obedience needs to be enforced with this divine command, and when the promise with which it is accompanied is a needed encouragement and support. If all parents were perfect and always dealt justly and kindly with their children, if they were always wise, and never made a mistake, it would be easy for a dutiful child, who is old enough to reason and act for himself, to yield prompt and unhesitating obedience; but there come occasions when against feeling, against conviction of expediency, with infinite self-denial, one must honor and obey. At such a time it has been found good, in a simple faith in this promise and a subordination of will to *God's* law to be filially obedient.

Human history has proven that this promise is to be relied upon. I may appeal to the observation and the experience of my readers; look around you, mark the boys and girls, now men and women, who when young were obedient and affectionate children; you will see them the prosperous and the prospered. However you may account for it, success seems to wait on the steps of a son or a daughter who honored father and mother. On the other hand, if you can remember disobedient sons and daughters, who by unkindness or even neglect, dishonored father and mother, you shall find, as you trace their history, that sooner or later, as if by an inevitable sequence, a blight has fallen on them and they have had an inheritance of disappointment and sorrow.

So clearly am I convinced of this law of God's providence, that I look for disaster to come by-and-by upon a son or a daughter who is recreant to filial duty; and all the more if the child has passed beyond the years of childhood and is still unfilial. The incentive appeals therefore not only to all the nobler and grateful instincts of one's nature, but to the clearest self-interest; the motive is not simply to please God, to pay a great debt which we lovingly recognize, but that we may have the smile of God upon our earthly lot—that our days may be prolonged and that it may go well with us in the land that the Lord God giveth us.

Let me, in what I have now to say to children, first address my remarks to those *who are still under the parental roof.* I need not linger long on the familiar thought that a son or daughter should be giving constantly honor and love to parents on whom they are dependent. It would seem that a natural instinct of manliness would prompt one to return at least these poor tributes. If any son or daughter can consent to receive a home and all the manifold good things which make the gift a blessing, can sit at the table, sleep in the bed, enjoy the fireside provided by kind parents, and still be undutiful and disobedient, I fear that no words of mine will have any force with him; a soul so thoroughly and intrinsically mean cannot be reached by any ordinary talk.

There is, however, even with the best son or daughter, a tendency to undervalue, at least at times a failure to rise to a full and clear appreciation of all that a parent is to a child. It is profitable for every child thoughtfully and deliberately to consider how much is due to a father and a mother. Common blessings are not always recognized. We do not know how blessed a thing this air is, nor how great a thing this sunshine is, and the all-surrounding air and sunshine of parental love are not understood. Take them away and you will then know. How often a child has only awakened to the value of a parent when he has looked upon father or mother lying before him in the silence of death!

Who shall tell adequately of the solicitude of which you have been the object, since first you opened your eyes upon this world? There were months together when your abject helplessness called out a wealth of love, and, in your infantile unconsciousness, you could not know it. And these were followed by years of watching and care. How many a day of weariness and anxiety; how many a night has been spent sleeplessly, walking with softened tread, or bending, with gushing tears, over the pillow where you lay with flushed cheek, moaning in your pain; how often have they gone into the busy street, forgetful of the crowd, because their hearts were full of forebodings for you, or have hastened nervously back again, to see if the hour, which was very long, had made any change in you. Nor have these sick times alone been those which have made you the objects of solicitude. Your whole life has been one perpetual calling of it forth. Your happiness has been the one end to which they have made all other things to bend. You can never understand it till you are parents yourselves.

Still, though you cannot now understand it all, yet frequently endeavor to appreciate what is so worthy of your earnest consideration. Think of it often, and you will see enough to call out your deepest gratitude.

But I will pass from these inner and tender

obligations to their outward manifestation. Let me say, then, to every child—*Show respect and honor to your parents.* I do not belong to the company of croakers who are perpetually mourning that the days when they were young were better than these degenerate times, and who find no good about them, but only deadness and rottenness in society; yet one can scarcely doubt that there is a general, wide-spread deficiency of true respect, not only for age, but even for parents themselves. It is, perhaps, an especial vice of this country, at least it is one that we are accused of by foreigners who have seen much of American society.

There are few boys and girls now-a-days, indeed, you might say, there are none at all—they are all either infants or men and women. The boy, scarce entered on his teens, is, in his own estimation, a full-grown man, capable of managing all his own affairs, and not standing in any need of the advice of that person whom he respectfully calls "the governor," or "the old gentleman." He keeps his own hours, chooses his own company, possibly makes his own purchases, though he may condescendingly permit his father to pay the bills. The girl, at the same mature age, grows wiser than her mother; rather deems it intrusive, certainly very annoying, to be asked about her last new acquaintance, who he is, or what is his character; thinks it all proper to have her mother attend to the state of her wardrobe and keep it in order, while she busies herself with what she calls "practising" in the parlor; to have the same good person glowing over her laces in the kitchen, or attending to the dinner which she will come down by and by to eat.

There are too many such children. Their irreverence and unfilial conduct are exhibited in a thousand ways. Let me exhort any child who reads this, to resolve never to yield, even for an instant, to this bad tendency of the times. Whatever others may be, determine that no word or look of yours shall ever give a suspicion that your father and mother are not enshrined in a sacred place in your soul. Never permit a word or a look to cause even a shadow of a fear to cross your parents' mind that you have anything but the deepest respect for them. I have incidently quoted one of the slang phrases by which a father, I would not say mother, is referred to.

No son and no daughter, with true filial honor in their souls will be guilty of using any of them—they are simply the evidence of reverence and honor gone. Do not be ashamed to say, under any circumstances, "Father!" "Mother!" Never consent to use any other word. If the company about you seem to make the terms out of place, it is no company for you. Where you cannot speak freely, and show by all that you say, that they are honored and loved, there you ought not to remain. It is pitiable, and very shameful, for a boy to hesitate to speak reverently of his father, or be unwilling to show that he is influenced by his mother. The moment any one of my young readers detects in himself the beginning of such a feeling, let him, with deepest indignation, rise against it and crush it out as a viper too loathsome to live a moment.

The failure of respect and honor, of which I am now speaking, as it is an indication, so also is it the result of a wandering away from the right path; and, where you discover it, you need not be surprised by and by to see a future clouded with deeper shades of crime.

Guard, then, the first beginnings of failing reverence; suffer nothing to lower the deep-toned honor which you habitually give your parents.

But more than this:—*Confide in your parents.* Make them, above all others, your confidants. They are the best and most disinterested friends you will ever have in this world. I do not deny that it is entirely natural for you to think that they do not and cannot, from the position of things, know much, at least very much, about your affairs, and that therefore you cannot talk confidentially with them. Do not, however yield to any such impression. Cultivate rather the habit of consultation with them. On things great and small seek their advice. A daughter will never come to shame, a son never to dishonor that does so.

Especially consult them in relation to your reading and your companions. Of the last, I will not say much. If, especially, a daughter can consent to make and keep an acquaintance without the knowledge of her parents, and contrary to their wishes, she silently declares that her moral principle is already shaken; she is not far from utter ruin. But I wish to speak of books. Let me say, with all the emphasis I am capable of using, to my young friends—Never read a book that you would not be willing your father or mother should see. I hope that no daughter who reads these pages would ever sully the purity of her soul by even glancing at an immoral book. I have too high a view of the beauty of your maiden life to think it possible; but I know what are the temptations which assail your brothers. There are circulated secretly, and in numbers greater than we often think, books which are emanations of the pit, reeking with licentiousness, and written to feed the most dangerous passions. Multitudes are all the while being ruined body and soul by them. I warn you against them. If you read them, you will never while you live be rid of the taint they leave on your nature. If they do not lead you to crime and loathsome disease and death, they will make agony for you in the coming time. Their pictures will live in your memory and grow vivid in your imagination; their words will whisper like fiends in your ear when you would give a world could you shut them out from sight and hearing; they will thrust themselves in upon your holiest hours; they will dog your steps; they will crawl over your soul with slimy trail, till in utter agony you cry out,

Who shall deliver me from this death? An hour may make the reading, a life-time will make the mourning over it.

If ever a companion puts a book in your hand and charges you to be careful that father or mother or sister does not see it, take the alarm. Turn from him as if you saw the white sore of leprosy upon his brow, as if you felt the breath of small-pox on your cheek. Worse than leprosy or small-pox is near you then!

Determine here and now—you do not know a thousandth part of the meaning of it—that you will never read a book of which mother does not know, or with which you would start or blush did she look over your shoulder while you read.

Confide, then, in your father and mother. There is to me something very beautiful in the intimacy of a father and a son, to see them walking side by side, perhaps arm in arm, in familiar converse on the street, the old man and the young in all the confidence of a hallowed friendship! It gives a satisfaction like a fair broad landscape at sunset. I know stalwart sons who to-day consult their mothers as in the days of yore, when they stood little higher than her knee—they are not low in my esteem, and I deem those mothers very happy in them.

There is an exquisite story of filial reverence in Herodotus. Crœsus, after displaying his wealth and magnificence to Solon, asked him who of all the men he had seen was the most happy? expecting of course that Solon would reply, Crœsus. But the philosopher spoke briefly of another. I will give the rest in the historian's own words:—"When Solon had roused the attention of Crœsus by relating many and happy circumstances concerning Telus, Crœsus expecting at least to obtain the second place, asked whom he had seen next to him. Cleobis, said he, and Biton, for they being natives of Argos possessed a sufficient fortune and had withal such strength of body that they were both alike victorious in the public games; and moreover, the following story is related of them: When the Argives were celebrating a festival of Juno, it was necessary that their mother should be drawn to the temple in a chariot; but the oxen did not come from the fields in time; the young men therefore being pressed for time, put themselves beneath the yoke and drew the car in which their mother sat; and having conveyed it forty-five stades, they reached the temple. After they had done this in sight of the assembled people, a most happy termination was put to their lives; and in them the Deity clearly showed that it is better for a man to die than to live. For the men of Argos, who stood around, commended the strength of the youths, and the women blessed her as the mother of such sons; but the mother herself, transported with joy, both on account of the action and its renown, prayed that the goddess would grant to Cleobis and Biton, her own sons, who had so highly honored her, the greatest blessing man could receive. After this prayer, when they had sacrificed and partaken of the feast, the youths fell asleep in the temple itself, and never woke more, but met with such a termination of life. Upon this, the Argives, in commemoration of their piety, caused their statues to be made and dedicated at Delphi."

Nor need we confine these thoughts wholly to sons. The beauty of intimacy between parent and child is not theirs alone. When does a daughter appear so attractive as when showing her love to father or mother, as when employed in some way lightening their cares or relieving their burdens? It would not be far from wrong were I to say to a young man who is looking with some degree of interest for a life-companion:—Would you know what kind of a wife she will make upon whom now you have your eye? Ask *what kind of a daughter she is now?* If she be indolently selfish, leaving care and work to her mother; especially if she be unloving or undutiful, beware of her; she is not likely to make you happy. If she be an affectionate and self-denying daughter, if she is intimate and confidential with her parents, you have in that the best promise of happiness in the future. The eye of mother or father, beaming with delight as it rests upon a daughter's form, moving lightly in their presence, is an unspoken recommendation of untold value.

But, whether the eye of friend or admirer is observing her or not, a daughter should cultivate this feeling of confidential intimacy with her parents; there is safety in it for her and unbounded happiness for them.

"Some feelings are to mortals given,
With less in them of earth than heaven;
And if there be a human tear,
From passion's dross refined and clear,

A tear so limpid and so meek,
It would not stain an angel's cheek,
'Tis that which pious fathers shed
Upon a duteous daughter's head!"

Let me say a few words to *children who have gone out from their old homes, but who have parents still.* There is always a liability, when sons and daughters have gone away from the home of their childhood, and have formed homes of their own, gradually to lose the old attachments and cease to pay those attentions to their parents which were so easy and natural in the olden time. New associations, new thoughts, new cares, all come in, filling the mind and heart, and, if special pains be not taken, they crowd out the old loves. This ought never to be. You should remember that the change is with you and not with those you left behind. You have every thing new, much that is attractive in the present and bright in the future; their hearts cling to the past, they have most in memory. When you went away, you knew not, and will never know till you experience it, what it cost them to give you up, nor what a vacancy you left behind. They have not, if you have, any new loves to take the place of the old. Do not, then, heartlessly deprive them of what you still can give of attention and love.

Visit your parents. If you live in the same place, let your step be, perhaps daily, a familiar one in the old home; if you are miles, yea, many miles away, make it your business to go to them. In this matter do not regard time nor expense; the one is well spent and the other will be fully, yea, a hundredfold repaid. When some day the word reaches you, flashed over the telegraph, that father or mother has gone, you will not think them much, those hours of travel which last bore you to their side.

Write to your parents. I have known father and mother wait with sick hearts through weary months, longing that some word might reach them from an absent son. They have watched the mails till in despair they have ceased to expect any more, and while they may not have the grief of a great bereavement, they have what is almost as bad, the bitter consciousness that they are not in mind enough even to call out a few poor lines from one whose infancy and early years they watched with sleepless love. Sons are often guilty of this crime—I cannot call it less—from sheer neglect or indolence. While an hour, perhaps a few moments, would suffice to write a letter which would give unspeakable satisfaction, they let months and even years slip away in utter indifference to all the pain they are causing. Oh, how full is many a mother's heart of sorrow and foreboding, when just a few words from an absent son would fill it with joy and praise! Such indifference or neglect is shameful and wicked. One need not wonder that sons guilty of it are not prospered, that they wait in vain for those turns of fortune which will send them home, as they dream, to surprise the old neighborhood with their wealth. Their thoughtlessness has been productive only of disaster.

Keep up your intercourse with father or mother; do not deem it sufficient to write when something important is to be told; do not say, "No news is good news." If it be but a few lines, write them; write, if it be only to say — "I am well," if it be only to send the salutation that says they are "dear," or the farewell that tells them that you are "affectionate" still. The little messengers shall be like caskets of jewels, and the tears that fall fondly over them will be treasures for you. Say with a warm-hearted son—

"The hills may tower, the waves may rise,
 And roll between my home and me;
Yet shall my quenchless memories
 Turn with undying love to thee!"

In the passing of human life there frequently comes a time when the mutual duties of child and parent are reversed. Advancing years bring a childhood to the one and the care of childhood to the other. To the aged father and mother the days of labor are over; the work of life has been done. Now attentive tenderness becomes the duty of those who once received it all themselves, while those are dependent upon it, who once gave it all. Now the parent is the child, and the child is the parent. The watchfulness and care of many years ago is to be repeated over again; only that the giver then, is the receiver now. To a true-hearted child here is a return of love which it is good to make. There is a deep satisfaction in being able to repay by words and looks the lavished love of the by-gone time.

If would be well if the return were always given. There is an old proverb, "One father can support ten children; ten children cannot support one father." It is one of those proverbs which, because they are true enough to become proverbs, make us ashamed of human nature. The thought here subtilly conveyed, is, no doubt, exaggerated, yet observation will too readily expose as true its foundatian. Though it is well said by Trench, from whom I quote it, "Seeing that it is the order of God's providence in the world that fathers should in all cases support children, while it is the exception when children are called upon to support parents, one can only admire that wisdom which has made the instincts of natural affection to run rather in the descending than in the ascending line;" yet it does not, it seems to me, take much from the humiliation which one feels as he is compelled to acknowledge the fact, that the return of parental affection comes so hard.

It is not, indeed, always easy, perhaps not, in some cases, possible for a child to return to a parent all the pious offices which once were given him; yet what more beautiful, what more lofty exhibition of filial tenderness and duty can be given than by a son or daughter waiting on an aged father or mother! It challenges your admiration.

It is not, however, seen every day. To some children — I can scarcely bring myself to speak of it — an aged parent seems to be in the way. I will not allude to the unspeakable meanness, the cruel and ungrateful wickedness that wishes them gone, that their property may come into possession. But who can tell of the soul-sorrows, and the secret but hot tears that flow down furrowed faces, making the evening of life full of bitterness, caused by this ill-concealed feeling that their presence is a burden? It is well that the old eyes are dim and the old ears heavy, for even now father and mother are made to fear that they have lingered too long on life's stage, and had better be gone.

I am aware that the care of an aged parent is not as easy nor as pleasant as that of a child; but who that has a spark of manhood or womanhood would refuse it, though it be not? No, no; when your steps falter, if they ever do, call up the olden time, the infant days; remember that there is no love like what they gave you then. It is only simple gratitude in you to return it now. Never hesitate; never refuse to do all, whatever it may be, that can make the evening's close sweet to them ; never by word or look give occasion for them to think that it is anything but good for you to wait upon them.

Remember that possibly you, too, may be old. I have seen a little story somewhere. Let me tell it to you. An aged father was living with a married son. The old man was far advanced in life ; his hand was unsteady, his eye dim, and he had long ago lost the trim neatness of earlier days. It was not pleasant for the family to see him at the table, feeding himself in his trembling and uncertain way ; so a wooden bowl, which he could not break, was provided for him, a spoon that he could handle, and a seat by the fire-place, where he could be no annoyance to any one. There, in his loneness, the old man would take meekly his meals, while children and grandchildren sat at the table. One day it happened that the father noticed his little son with a knife cutting diligently into a piece of wood, intently fashioning something. He carelessly asked, "What, my boy, are you making?" The little fellow, keeping still on with his work, with the unconscious frankness of childhood, replied, "I 'm making a trough to feed papa out of when he gets old."

It was enough. The child-word was a revelation.

But we ought never to need that argument, addressed, as it is, to our self-interest—the argument to be faithful because we may need a similar care; rather let it spring forth—the glad tribute of filial love. Let the language of Pope express our thought:—

> "Me, let the tender office long engage
> To rock the cradle of reposing age;
> With lenient arts extend a mother's breath,
> Make languor smile, and smooth the bed of death;
> Explore the thought, explain the asking eye,
> And keep awhile one parent from the sky."

Ye privileged children! Ye who have yet a father or a mother spared to you, I charge you to have some true appreciation of a blessing whose value you can never know till it has been forever withdrawn. You will have, you can have but one mother, one father. No one will ever love you as they have loved. By and by they will be gone. You will stand over them as they lie still in death; memory will be very busy, then, and very unsparing; yes, and very partial. She will bring up, not so much the good and loving deeds of the past, but more than all else, the unkind and the undutiful. Every look of disrespect, every unaffectionate word, every disobedient act, will come out of the dim past, and, pointing to the dead, will charge home your guilt. Then you would give a world if you could only speak in that ear your prayer for forgiveness and a parent's blessing;—but it will be too late. "What would I not give," said Charles Lamb, "to call my dear mother back to earth for a single day, to ask her pardon, upon my knees, for all those acts by which I grieved her gentle spirit."

> "'Tis only when the lips are cold,
> We mourn with late regret,
> 'Mid myriad memories of old,
> The days forever set;
> And not an act, or look, or thought
> Against thy meek control,
> But, with a sad remembrance fraught,
> Wakes anguish in my soul!"

Now, while these parents live, be all that you can be to them. Give love for their love. It will be a satisfaction simply unspeakable by and by that you did. Some are old. They linger awhile below, often lonely, often sad, sometimes wishing, in their sadness and loneliness, that they were gone; they are looking forward to heaven to restore what they have lost. By your loving words and gentle acts make the lost seem little as you may; let their nearness to heaven make them sacred in your eyes:—

> "As one by one they enter in, and the stern portals close once more,
> The halo seems to linger round those kneeling closest to the door."

Others live in their ripened maturity. Make ye much of them. Honor, love them more and more as your life glides on. May their last look have for you in it a smile and a benediction!

CHAPTER VII.

BROTHERS AND SISTERS.

Love as brethren.—1 PETER. iii. 8.

"But are they speaking, singing, yet, as in their days of glee?
Those voices, are they lovely still, still sweet on earth or sea?
Oh, some are hushed and some are changed, and never
shall one strain
Blend their fraternal cadences triumphantly again."
HEMANS.

THE family is like a delicate piece of mechanism; every part of it has its place and function, and when all is in harmonious adjustment it moves noiselessly and does its work well. But if even a small nut be loose, especially if a lever be out of time or a rod be bent, you hear noise, feel the jar, the work is spoiled, and by and by the whole machine is racked and comes to a stand. Father and mother may be in harmony, and like the motive power keep all in action, but the brothers and sisters of the household are parts of the engine and will make or mar its work.

Have you never noticed how little a thing will destroy, for a whole day, the quiet movement of a family? One member of it has "got out of bed," as our mothers used to say, "on the wrong side," and either from some nervous derangement or other physical cause, feels "out of sorts;" or because he has been crossed in something, or has the discomfort of a troubled conscience, or from what you can only call, *pure badness,* he contrives to make himself generally disagreeable. He does unpleasant things, says ugly ones, is selfish and annoying. Such an one will spoil the moments of family prayer, take away the appetite for breakfast, and throw a silence and gloom over a whole family circle, and yet have done nothing very positively wicked. He has only been a little while out of gear. On the other hand, how the smile and bright voice of a little child chases away the gathered frowns and makes sunshine, as it bursts into the room where things were just now growing cloudy, perhaps stormy!

If each brother and sister would but understand their place in the adjustments of the family life, and each be bringing the best of work and play to increase its joys, homes would grow harmoniously beautiful where often all is gloom and deformity. It is not wealth nor even competence that makes a home fair; no, not that, but sunny looks, loving words and kindly acts.

I want to say some things to brothers and sisters, and in doing so shall take the opportunity of speaking, in general, to young people on matters which touch their associations together.

Boys and girls are not the same. They are born different and show it while they are infants. The boy-baby is restless and uneasy in his mother's arms. He is never still except when asleep, and even then tumbles from side to side in his crib with sudden flings of arms and legs. When he grows beyond babyhood he plays differently. Without ever being told of it, he instinctively turns away from dolls; lays them aside in indifference, and freely donates them to whatever little girl will have them. He demands balls and bats and drums; he turns down chairs for horses, lays hold on all the strings of the house for lines, wants all the little sticks made into whips, mounts lounges and drives four in hand; he asks for guns, and wants you tell him stories of bears and lions and tigers, and is amused beyond measure at their leaping upon and eating up cows and oxen. The girl-baby is gentle, even from the first, and looks quietly out of the blue eyes, or laughingly out of the dark ones. She takes naturally to her dolls, and never wearies of dressing them and arranging the baby-house; she is gentle in her plays, and would be frightened with what would fill her brother with a paroxysm of delight; she loves fairy tales and will not laugh and ask some absurd question about the babes in the wood, but rather cries over their sorrows. The sister will smoothe pussy and hold her lovingly in her lap, while the brother wants to see if the cat can jump, and when she tries to get out of his undesirable company, will detain her by the leg or tail. And these same divergencies of disposition and character perpetuate themselves as the boy or girl grows older. There are exceptions, it is true; some boys have all the tastes and gentleness of a feminine nature, and some girls have much that is masculine. I do not regret seeing it in each. The gentle boy will not make any the less noble man because there was so much that was girl-like in his childhood, nor will the girl that was, in her rudeness, often called a boy, be any the less, but perhaps all the more a true and lovely woman.

These innate differences of disposition in brothers and sisters must always be taken into the account, in the family. They demand mutual forbearance and sympathy. The sisters are not to expect all gentleness and propriety in their brothers. They must make up their minds to be often fretted and annoyed by shouts and noise, even if they are not made to suffer now and then by thoughtless mischief. Brothers must remember, that what may be good and excellent fun for them, may be only injury and wrong to a sister whose nature is so contrary to theirs.

When, however, in a family these different characteristics are properly understood and adjusted, they tend largely to the development of character. They affect healthfully each other. A sister ought to be a wiser and a better sister for having had a brother, and he is a bad brother who is not purer and better and nobler for having had a sister.

Brothers and sisters ought to *hold each other's affection*. I know that love is natural between them, but I know too, that the love is very often lost as the years go on. You have seen it perhaps, more than once—brothers and sisters who spent their childhood under the same roof, as they grew to be men and women gradually having less and less to do with one another, and, even if no positive quarrel has put them wholly asunder, by-and-by almost losing track of each other's history. This is both wrong and sad. The experiences of childhood and youth ought to make it impossible. In these years the links of a chain may be forged and welded that not the rust of time, nor the fret and strain of life shall break or even weaken.

Cultivate a cordial and loving sympathy with each other, and permit nothing to drift you apart. As no kind brother would wantonly break his sister's doll or over-set her tea-table, and as no good sister would refuse to make a cover for her brother's ball or a bag to hold his marbles; so as they grow older, let each endeavor to enter into the pursuits and feelings of the other. The brother will be in store or workshop or college, the sister, will be at home, each moving in different scenes and associations, but let them day by day try to pass, each the boundary of the other's domain and in it be at home.

Confide in each other, and *be intimate with each other.* I do not deem it a beautiful thing when a sister is ready to make a confidant of almost any one rather than her brother; nor for a brother to be more intimate and confidential with almost any one's sister rather than his own. There should be such an interest shown each in the other that they will be ready mutually to speak and consult about things which would be confided tô no one else. In the unselfish intimacy of their life they can help each other as can no one else. A sister may get the counsel and the help of a brother, when she can, perhaps, properly seek it from no other male friend; and a brother may avail himself of the womanly tact and instinct of a sister, when no other lady friend can be called to his assistance.

Sisters, do not turn off your younger brothers as if they were always in your way, and any service which they might ask of you were a burden. Perhaps the hour may come when, over a coffin that looks strangely longer than you thought, and over a pale brow where often, half unwillingly and perhaps with a petulent push, you parted the hair; you bend with blinding tears and sobs that shake your very soul, while remorseful memory is busy with the bygone hours. You will wish then, that when he came and asked you to help him in his play, or to lift him on your lap because he was tired, or take him out because he wanted to see, you had laid aside your book and made the little heart glad.

There is that in the very name of sister which is precious. A sister's love! It goes back to infantile hours, it looks over days of childhood's innocence. Perhaps it speaks of the little crib where brother and sister in the olden time lay their two fair heads on the pillow side by side and slept with hands in each other's, as only children sleep after a day's play; it tells of days when they waded in brooks, when they built houses, sat by little tables and drank tea out of tiny cups, and then went to play-homes arm-in-arm; of evenings when they knelt at mother's knee and wanted each the last kiss for good-night; of later days when they went side by side to school, and told, round the table at evening, school experiences; or when they drew each other over the smooth snow with many a shout, or came home tired but merry with skates hanging by long straps over the shoulder! Oh, there are many scenes which you hardly notice now, that will come up in all their vividness by and by; and what I want is, that you should make them now such that, in the time to come when they are fixed in memory, and when neither line nor shadow can be changed, they shall be only bright and beautiful. Boys and girls, you are painting now, and the canvas is not frail, nor will the colors fade; by and by the pictures shall be hung up in memory's hall and you cannot but gaze upon them. Paint them, then, so that in that coming time they shall give you only delight. Do the kind and loving deeds, speak the pleasant words; they will come back to soothe your heart when, some day, it is almost bursting with grief.

The polite attentions of a brother and sister touch me, when my attention would not be caught by the same things from others. These attentions should always be given. A brother should never permit a sister to want an escort or be dependent on the attentions of any friend. A sister should feel that she has, in her brother, one to whom not only she may look, in time of danger or trouble, for protection, but one whose care over her makes her independent of every one else. I once heard a sister say, "I never asked my brother to go anywhere with me and had him refuse;" and I deemed it a crown on the head of that brother, just as I knew it was said with a glow of sisterly pride and exultation.

In children

> "There is seen
> The baby figures of the giant mass
> Of things to come at large."

The boys and girls are what the men and women will be by and by. The good sisters make the good wives, and the good brothers make the good husbands of the after time. If you want to know with a fair certainty what each will be in the unalterable relation and solemn responsibilities of married life, you can see it all mirrored in the life that as child and youth they led. The affectionate kindness, considerate attention and unselfish devotion which made brother and sister dear to each other, and made the home calm and beautiful, will not have exhausted themselves when the old home is left, but on nearer and dearer ones will pour out their treasures of grace and goodness.

Ye who woo! Ye who are sought! Beware ye of the son or the brother who was cold-hearted, selfish or neglectful! Beware ye of the daughter or sister who, as such, failed to be loving and kind!

Sisters, *guard and protect your brothers.* You wonder that I say so to you. The guard and the protection, you think, should surely rather come from them. But there is a talismanic power, which may emanate from a fragile and gentle sister, mightier than brawny muscle or iron will. A sister can throw over her brother the purity of her maiden life, which shall surround him like a charmed atmosphere. Oh, if some sisters had understood this, and had won and held their brothers to their side; if they had but shown them the beauty and the grace; had made to pass not only before them, but to touch and caress them lovingly, the sweetness and the spotless innocence of a true woman's life, they would have clad their brother in a panoply of steel, and put in his hand a weapon whose very gleam would have scared away the ugly demons of vice and infamy. But they did not do it; and so he went out, and wanton and brazen-faced temptation, not put to shame by the contrast of love and purity at home, easily gained the victory over him. Try, then, to live so lovingly and with such power that, when vice allures your brother, there shall come up such visions of purity and affection, that, in the contrast, he shall turn in disgust and loathing away.

Let brothers *protect the reputation and the happiness of their sisters.* Do not think me saying only something stale and commonplace. It would be commonplace if I meant only that a brother should defend his sister's honor. If he would not do that, let him lay aside the name of brother. I mean much more than that. Let him make a defence in her own bosom, by daily exhibiting before her the ideal of a man, pure, honorable and good. Then, when one stained and dishonorable comes near her, the ideal shall help her intuition, and he shall have no power over her.

Let a brother also make a wall about his sister, so that she shall be shielded from the contact of all but the pure and good. You, as a young man, may have been thrown into companionship with one whom you know to be impure and licentious, and he may seek the acquaintance of your sister. Let him seek it in vain! Let the harlots with whom he has been in fellowship suffice him; never let his presence pollute the air which your sister breathes; never let his touch defile your sister's hand!

Nor need I confine what I want to say to brothers alone. Let sisters protect themselves. "Why did you not take my brother's arm last night?" asked a young lady of her friend, a very intelligent girl of eighteen or nineteen." "Because," was the reply, "I knew him to be a licentious young man." "Nonsense," the sister said; "if you refuse the attentions of all licentious men you will have none." "Very well, then, I can dispense with them altogether." There was a volume of revelation in the brief conversation.

Young women are not always true as they ought to be to themselves. Frequently a man is known to be immoral; perhaps known to have been the betrayer of one who fatally put her trust in his honor, and whom he ruined forever; and yet that man is welcomed into the society of the pure, as if there were no stain upon his soul and no crime cursing the ground on which he treads. The wretch who could deliberately plot, and steadily accomplish, the destruction of a young character and life, is not fit to walk even this sin-defiled earth. Instead of allowing such a being to associate in familiar friendship with you, you should stand for your honor, defend the sanctity of your life, keep untarnished your own purity, by banishing him from your presence. You should have enough of sisterhood in your heart to avenge the immeasurable wrong he has done your sister-woman. The patriot would loathe the hand of a traitor, much more should you disdain a worse than traitor's touch.

Let brothers and sisters, whatever else they do, keep pure the air of home. Ye brothers, see that no serpent leaves its slimy trail, or even crosses the grass upon which your sister walks.

Girls do not always know their power. It is far greater than they think; and were they true and brave enough to exert it, they might almost, in a generation, revolutionize society about them. Exert your power for good upon the young men who are privileged to enjoy your society. Gentle and good, I need not exhort you to be. Be brave and true. Try *to exhibit the ideal of a woman*—a pure and good woman—whose life is mighty as well as beautiful in its maidenly dignity and attractive loveliness. Do not let it even seem that dress and frivolity make your only thoughts; but let the elevation of your character, and the usefulness of your life, lift up the man that walks by your side. Some of you are in intimate associations, which, under exchanged promises, look forward to a nearer and more enduring relation. In these hours do nothing to lower, but everything to refine and ennoble each others' character. Young girl, not a christian, beware how you draw aside or weaken the piety of the young man who seeks your society and your heart. Every church privilege neglected, every inconsistent thing done at your solicitation, may be a thorn planted in your pillow by and by. Rather be yourself a christian and throw over the days of courtship the hallowed power of prayer, of holy thoughts and a devoted life; be—

"A perfect woman, nobly planned,
To warn, to comfort and command;
And yet a spirit still and bright
With something of an angel light."

I have been all along speaking to brothers and sisters in their relation to each other; let me say a few things to brothers alone. It is too sadly true that the injunction, "Love as brethren," would, in many cases, convey the idea of no very admirable kind of love. Brothers quarrel and annoy one another in early life, and then, by and by, when once the forced associations of home are broken up, have nothing more to do with one another. Never permit this so to be.

While you are together, now, as boys, stand together. I do not mean simply as against those who would harm you. A brother who would not, according to his ability, fight for his brother, does not deserve the name of one. But I mean, help each other in the home. Be ready to lend a hand at a hard lesson or a difficult job; and if some self-denial of yours can promote your brother's comfort and enjoyment, be not too selfish to give it. And do not permit your boyish habits of teasing to make you only a nuisance in the house, while the house itself is in peace only when the brothers, like mischievous animals, are in separate rooms.

Stand, brothers, together in the whole future of your life. You remember the ancient fable of the old father and his sons with the bundle of sticks. He called his children round him just before his death, and taking a number of rods closely bound together, handed them to his sons, telling them to break them. They tried with many a hard effort, but failed, and gave them back. The father then untied the bundle, and, passing out the rods one by one, commanded his sons now to break them. This was very easily done; rod after rod snapped under even a gentle pressure. The lesson was there:—As brothers, they were to stand together, and have multiplied strength as they stood.

Brothers, alas! too often step out from their boyhood home and at once forget the old ties; they seem more willing to lend a helping hand to others, who have no such claim, than to brothers with whom their earliest days were spent. There is a power in the mutual help made by this standing side by side. I have now in mind three brothers, all men of large prosperity and extensive influence, and both prosperity and influence almost wholly due to the help which each brother lent the other. They went hand in hand in the christian life, the oldest amid tears of gratitude and joy, pointing the younger brother, in his agony, to the Saviour of sinners. They have gone hand in hand ever since. The elder was successful in business and, with his advancement, he laid hold on and lifted his brother with him. They two, the one loaning and pledging all the property he had, and the other, with larger pledges, all that was needed, gave the third capital, which in a few years produced a vast return, with independent wealth and widening influence. Each of the three rejoices in his brother's success and good name as if they were his own.

One of the great inventions which will make the first half of this century forever memorable, and which has enrolled its author as one of the benefactors of the race, would probably never have been perfected by the brain that wrought it out, had not the arm of a brother held firmly up the inventor in the days of experiment and unappreciated and unrewarded toil.

A friend once told me in the intimacy of friendship, that years before he had lent his brother the most of all he was worth, and that he had lost it all. " But," he added, " I am not sorry; I would do it again if I had it." A fine ideal of brotherhood was in the utterance.

Who is there that you should stand by, if not your brother?—the brother with whom you slept and played in the by-gone time, whose very life was a part of your mother's life and love! Never permit a family quarrel to separate you. I know well how brothers and sisters are sometimes sundered forever. Petty questions of property, even a piece of old furniture, fit only for the junk shop, has been enough to dash into fragments the associations of childhood and remove forever from each other's side brothers and sisters, whom nothing but death should have divided. This could never have come to pass, if from the first they had loved and clung to one another. If there ever, and there may easily, come a time when some selfish interest of yours breaks in, and there seems a danger that by it brother or sister may be wounded or withdrawn from the circle, do you push it aside! Call up all the love of the early time and say, "Nothing, nothing shall turn my brother's heart away." Oh, there is a joy which swells the heart and brims the eye as you look back over the years which have held brothers and sisters to your side! There are few more beautiful greetings than the warm kisses and tight hand-claspings of brothers and sisters. I have had them in the home and across the desk, in a busy counting-room after months of absence, and they live more than pictures now in memory, realities that throw their light and heat over the abyss of years.

Perhaps some of you, while you read, know all I mean, and your hearts respond in joy that such experiences have been yours. I give you my congratulations. Some of you read this with only a pang of remorseful regret, while accusations and excuses make tumult within your hearts. I pity you. May God forgive you, if you have been in fault. If brother and sister have not gone forever, try to gather up the broken links and weld them together again with tears and loving words.

Keep up your associations with each other. When you have gone from the old home, when it itself has passed away, visit each other's homes, and do not consider either time or money wasted in the journey. Write to each other. I know brothers and sisters who have been, perhaps, a score of years away from the old home circle, and have through them all, week by week, exchanged letters, usually having more than enough to say, till the communication has grown into a habit, and each would be unhappy were it broken up. The weekly letter is welcomed and prized beyond any thing else that the mails contain.

Perhaps some boy or girl is reading this—Let me counsel you, as sisters and brothers, to stand together and to love each other. Boys, be kind and gentle to your sisters; sisters, be patient and forbearing with your brothers; brothers, go side by side in life's work and battle. Now, while you are boys together, be good and true to one another, and in all the coming time let nothing part you. A continent may be between you, but let your affection span the rivers, float over the mountains and plains, ethereal, but more lasting than time and stronger than all the changes of earth.

CHAPTER VIII.

THE EMPLOYER AND THE EMPLOYED.

Honor all men.—1 PETER ii. 17.

Gathering from the pavement's crevice as a floweret of the soil,
The nobility of labor—the long pedigree of toil.
LONGFELLOW.

SINCE the world has stood men have been divided into two classes—the employers and the employed—those who have used the service of others, and those who have rendered service. I say two classes, and yet when you attempt to draw a line between them, you will find it impossible, since the one passes perpetually over into the domain of the other. Here you have a capitalist who has a thousand men in his service; but he himself is employed by each one who deals with him in his line of business, whether it be the man who engages him to build a ship, or the purchaser who buys a yard of goods in his acre-covering establishment. The employer who has just now paid wages to the servant in his household, goes to his counting-room and there receives his compensation for services which he has rendered to another. Thus from the millionaire down to the humblest laborer this rendering service and receiving wages interlaces and crosses, so that you can hardly tell off the respective companies.

While, however, human society remains what it is, and while men differ in talent, disposition and character, there always will be those who are especially employed at more or less fixed and regular compensation for services which they give to others; and there will be another class who use and pay for such services. While it may be impossible, theoretically and with accuracy, to make the demarcation, yet the fact that there is and always will be such a division, is sufficiently clear to every one.

These too classes are so related that they are and must be mutually dependent. The highest and the lowest in social position are here so intimately connected that the happiness and well-being of each is in the hands of the other. The millionaire may have his equanimity destroyed by his cook, and the capitalist be ruined by the clerk to whose salary he scarcely gives a thought. "The head cannot" here "say to the foot, I have no need of thee."

Still, though there be this inter-penetration of interests and dependency, there *is* a head and there *is* a foot in the social system. The providence of God, overruling the appointments of life, has made it necessary that some must occupy the subordinate places. Not simply the happiness of society, but even its very existence depends on it. If everybody were an employer, when would the work be done? If every one were on the quarter-deck, the boiler fires would go out in the hold; if every one were architect and master builder, it would be long before the foundation trench would be dug or the wall be reared; if every one were in the parlor, there would be some hungry mouths in the household.

The mental characteristics of the largest class of society make it simply a necessity that they should be employed by others. They neither desire nor have they, by their own acknowledgment and consciousness, the ability to control business for themselves. They would be neither happy nor prosperous if they did. If the day-laborer, whom you see toiling under the eye and according to the direction of a foreman, were made his own master, to do work independently, how long, think you, would it be before he would starve? You could do him confessedly no greater injury than to compel him to make plans and lay out schemes of work for himself. I have known men who have been employed as journeymen, contentedly, happily and prosperously for thirty or forty years in the same factory, who would have been ruined over and over again had they done business on their own account. They have had offers of business which their own good sense led them to decline; a rare self-appreciation gave them a wise choice. They were made for the places which they occupy, and they have filled them well, to their own honor and profit; both of which would have been sacrificed had they forced themselves into higher positions.

It would be well for those who sometimes are fretted and discontented at the different arrangements of life, especially as they regard the distribution of wealth, to consider, that were the respective positions of the capitalist and the laborer to be reversed, and all the property to be taken from the custody of the one and put into the hands of the other, this state of things could not continue. In a very brief period the whole case would change, and surprisingly soon the wealth would be seen to have slipped out of the hands of the last into those of the former owner, and the old relation of things would be re-established. By an arbitrary decree the employer might be made the employed, but as soon as the natural law prevailed, each would take his former place. There must, therefore, always be this mutual relation of which I am speaking.

All this declares the true and honorable position of labor. It is a foolish and very false notion that any labor, in itself right, can be at all degrading. "By the sweat of thy face shalt thou eat bread," was the allotment at the first, and those beaded drops of honest toil are the true jewels of manhood. Fashion adds to the folly in this matter, and often inflicts an endless amount of harm, by making one kind of labor respectable, and another humiliating.

A girl will attempt to make her living by the needle, and hurries herself to the grave in the endeavor, while as a domestic in some family greatly needing such services as hers, she might have a healthful home, free from care or privation; a young man toils amid poverty and anxiety in a clerkship, when a farm or a workshop beckons him to independence and competency. No, we should all settle this in our hearts—That man is noble, and that woman dignified, who discharges God-given duty well.

> "Honor and shame from no condition rise;
> Act well your part, there all the honor lies."

The corrupt official in his palace, luxuriating in his plundered gains, is base beside the honest street-sweeper who earns what he receives and fills the working hours with righteous toil. The man who, contented with his lot, meets the duty of the hour, ennobles whatever work he does, and walks a king in his realm of duty.

He only looks upon life correctly who sees God's hand in its appointments. This it is which gives the teachings of the Bible the aspect which they have :—" Servants, be obedient to them that are your masters . . . . as unto Christ; not with eye-service as men-pleasers, but as the servants of Christ, doing the will of God from the heart, ... with good will doing service, as to the Lord, and not to men. And ye masters do the same things unto them." Phil. vi. 5–7, 9. The Christian is to look upon the position which he holds and the work he is set to do as given him by Christ, his master, to do and hold for Him. At once, the service becomes no longer low or menial, whatever it may be, but honorable, since it is done for Him. An angel would probably make very little account of what kind of work he was sent to do, and would quite as joyfully and readily sweep Wall Street, as sell stocks in one of its decorated offices.

These precepts, given in this light, make clear the way in which our work should be done for those who employ us—not as under the eye of a task-master, but only under the eye of The Infinite Master, to gain first, and above all others His approbation. This thought will make smooth many a rough place, and help us tide over those rocky ones which meet us so frequently in life. If all employers were kind and uniformly considerate, if they were never unreasonable and never were mistaken, if they were never perplexed and never had to alter a plan, and if we always understood exactly what they wished and always knew precisely how they wished it done, and could do it on the moment, even when something else were to be done at the same time, then all the sailing would be plain. But it is not so, and this makes necessary patience, forbearance and good-nature on the part of the employed. To this a Christian spirit, which endeavors chiefly to please the Saviour, will greatly help us.

The employed should cultivate *Good nature.* That disposition which leads one to sing while doing her work, which makes a man whistle at his task, which helps him to be silent and not answer back when unjustly faulted, to be calm and neither sullen nor sulky, even when imposed on, is better than thousands of gold, for it does and purchases what gold cannot get or do.

The employed should *give the whole of his time and his skill* during the hours for which his service has been engaged. It is simply dishonest, for one to idle away the time of his employer, or to be neglectful or careless of the manner in which his work is done. These hours and this skill are not his but another's. Have you never seen a man, and been interested as you have looked, stand leaning on the handle of his hammer while he talked across the bench to another, who sat on it with his plane in his hand, as if the words they were speaking were too mighty to be interrupted by the stroke or push of either? Have you never seen a good worker, with thoughts evidently on everything else but her work, make terrific fits of the garments, or spoil the carefully selected dinners that had been sent home? Have you never known a waspish or complaining letter to come back from the purchaser because his bill of goods had been so badly made up, the articles which he wanted most left out, and the footings-up all wrong; because the clerk, in his lazy indifference, had failed to do his duty? I have heard of just such things in my time.

To attempt any detail of duty as it touches this relation would carry us beyond the limits of a single chapter. I propose rather, to give what seem to me, one or two plain and far-reaching principles which underlie it. There should be an *identification of interest* between the employer and employed. One of the most perplexing and important questions of the present time, is the relation between capital and labor. There is a class of men who make it their business to create and propagate the belief that there is a natural and necessary antagonism between the two interests. It will be noticed, if I am not mistaken, that this class is not usually composed of workingmen themselves. They are ex-workmen. They hold the high offices in the "Associations" or "Unions," and sometimes have salaries for their services; they have occasion to travel much on visitations to other associations; they are very busy, so that factories or shops do not have much of their services. The can talk well about "the rights of labor," and the oppression of the "rich who live in marble palaces," and all that sort of thing. Their chief stock in trade is the ignorance and prejudices of others; I had about written, their fellows, but they are not fellow-workmen at all; rather they derive support in their idleness out of the hard-working men, whose weaknesses they cunningly play upon.

Such men do an immeasurable amount of mischief. Emphatically, "idle and busy bodies," they are perpetually sowing discontent and making hardship where all ought to be harmony and prosperity.

There is no natural antagonism between capital and labor. The employer is not the inherent enemy of the employed, and whoever he be who teaches that he is, is either ignorant or a demagogue. The very constitution of society, as we have seen, makes necessary these two classes; they are mutually and absolutely dependent on each other, and neither can do without the other. Can you say that two deadly enemies are absolutely necessary to each other's happiness? That two, who perpetually and by necessity are trying to steal from each other, are vitally important to each other's prosperity? No, capital is the natural friend and support of labor; labor is the support and friend of capital. They are intended to build up each other's interests, and when rightly adjusted they always do. Whenever each acts with a fair consideration of the other's interests, all settles itself into uniform prosperity and mutual helpfulness. If the christian, Bible rule were carried into business relations, all the friction would soon be gone.

The identification of which I speak, should be equal on both sides. The employed should consider the interests of his employer his own. The advancement of the one is the success of the other. Self-interest, were there no higher motive, points out the true course. The men who rise to the higher places, are those who have discharged their duty best in the lower. They claim the better positions because they have made themselves so necessary, that their services cannot be dispensed with. "Seest thou a man diligent in his business? He shall stand before kings," is the Scripture proverb, and its truth is seen in all situations in life.

And here let me say to the employed:—*Aspire to higher places.* I remember an incident related to me by an acquaintance years ago, of Stephen Girard, the millionaire of Philadelphia. The old man met my friend, then a boy, sweeping out the entry of the store early one morning, and stopped to ask him some questions about his work and himself. Looking kindly at him, probably interested in the boy's intelligence and replies, he asked: "Do you intend always to be a hired man, my son?" "No," was the answer, "I intend and hope some day to be in business for myself!" "I applaud that!" benignantly said the old man, in his French way, laying his hand on his shoulder. It was kindly said, and gives a pleasant glimpse of a heart which was often thought cold and rugged, while it made an impression for good which, as my friend told me, had never been effaced. Take the wise lesson. Aspire to the higher places, and leave those you now have for other beginners. Aspire, but remember that you shall win them only by present content, and by doing faithfully what you now have in hand. *You reach them only because you have more than filled* your present place. If, because you think yourself too good or too big for it, you decline its duties, you will simply demonstrate your unfitness for it; the shrinkage will appear, and you will slip into a smaller and a smaller place. In the long run, and for the most part, men are found in the places they have fitted themselves to fill. Aspire and look forward to independent positions; but only by rounding out and overloading present duties.

Employers should identify themselves with those in their employ. There are many who seem to look upon the services of those engaged by them precisely as they would look upon those of a horse or an ox, except that the man may bring more intellect or intelligence to the work than the brute. They feel that their whole duty has been discharged when the stipulated wages have been paid; that when once the hired person has left store or factory, all connection with him has ceased, only to be renewed when the hour of work has come again. This should not be, and with a multitude of honorable employers it is far different.

The man or woman that works for you has, it may be, a wife and children at home; father and mother and brothers and sisters may be there, and so all the tremulous anxieties and tender sympathies, too, are there, which you can have in the same relations. He has sensibilities growing out of them that can be touched, and that will vibrate joyously or sadly under your hand. It would do you good and would do them good were you sometimes to go into the homes of your employés. You do not know how cheery and how strengthening it would be to them. Consider that your employés have feelings which can be wounded. They are not, because they are hired by you, made of cast iron, so that you may say and do what you will and not hurt them. No right minded man or woman will ever say or do anything wantonly to injure the feelings and inflict pain on any one, and especially on one who by his position cannot resent it. "Honor all men" is the pregnant word of the Bible, and it means — have correct and lofty views of every one with whom you come in contact. View the person, however humble, and however dependent, as a brother man or sister woman; with thoughts and feelings very much like yours; one that can suffer and can be glad. Remember that here you often hold the cords of suffering or of gladness in your hand.

Pay what is honest and fair. It is neither honest nor fair to endeavor to have services for less than what you know they are worth. Dishonesty is found not only with the cook or chamber-maid or porter or clerk, but also in the parlor and the back office; and many an employer, because he gets such excellent help at so small a price, deems himself shrewd and sharp, when he is only mean and dishonest. Pay what you believe the service ought to have.

Those who hire are often in serious error here. We sometimes expect the best sort of service for the poorest sort of wages. The great law of economics prevails in the household as elsewhere. If you want a good watch, a good coat, a fine book, you expect to pay a corresponding price. Cheap things are usually such only in name. Precisely so in labor. The more skill and ability, the higher the price.

Yet frequently this unfailing law is entirely ignored in the family. Honesty, integrity, skill, strength, politeness, and refinement even are sought but never found. The mistress is involved in perpetual worry, fret and annoyance; complains evermore of the incompetency of servants, but never gets at the true reason. She is not willing, or is not able to pay the wages which will insure the thing she requires. If we be not able to pay for the best goods, we must content ourselves with those of inferior quality. If we cannot pay for the highest style of culinary art, let us be content, happy if we can get a joint well roasted. There was a whole world of philosophy in the reply of an old colored servant. His master was blaming him for his neglects and the badness of his work. When he had done, the old man looked up and said, "Look 'ere, massa, you musn't expect to get the Angel Gabriel on five dollars a month."

Pay regularly and promptly what is due to your employés. Read some Scriptures on this point:— "The wages of him that is hired shall not abide with thee all night until the morning." Lev. xix. 13. "Woe unto him that useth his neighbor's service without wages, and giveth him not for his work." Jer. xxii. 13. "I will be a swift witness against the sorcerers and against the adulterers, and against the false swearers and"—note the company—"against those that oppress the hireling in his wages." Mal. iii. 5.

What may seem to be a very small thing to you, may, in reality, be a very great thing to one whose whole living it makes. Indifference and thoughtlessness in this thing frequently cause an amount of pain which no man or woman should be willing to inflict. Because the prompt payment of the daily wages may involve a momentary inconvenience, perhaps a mere breaking through a prescribed routine, or even because it may interrupt a conversation, with scarcely thought enough to look the creditor in the face, the debtor—just as truly a debtor as if the man or woman were asking a million—cries out, "Call again." He complacently turns to his paper or to his talk, as if he had done no wrong. He has committed a crime. He has sent that man away sad at heart to his home. He has compelled him to see his family deprived of necessities, perhaps put to suffering; he has forced him to make excuses to his own creditors with shame of face; to endure the feeling of wrong and helpless indignation, simply because, for some small reason, he has chosen to deprive a brother man of his rightful dues. All this is shamefully wrong; and, what is solemnly to be considered by such persons is, that God is offended by it, and they need not wonder if He who cares for the poor shall deal with them for it. They may deem it a small thing; but it is not small in His sight, and shall not escape His visitation.

Employers—and now I have reference particularly to those who have young men under their charge—should take *a deep interest in the moral character* of those in their employment. He who has taken a young man under his charge should take a broad view of the responsibility. He should feel a kindly care over him, and endeavor, by his influence, to strengthen and better his character.

It is to be feared that, in these days, employers do not make sufficient account of *Character*. They look for brightness, quickness and business ability, and are willing to pay for them, but put a small money value on integrity, honor and religion; and, it would seem, in making an engagement, leave all these latter qualifications entirely out of the account. So much is this so, that I have known it said, with a feeling of profound chagrin and disappointment, "These people seem to care nothing, and it goes for nothing whether a man is a good man or not." Perhaps the whole business world feels the subtle power of this thing. Men are trained to consider business tact, shrewdness and energy the only things of consequence; that, if a man be successful, he has done everything well.

If a different view should be taken, and, from the first, young men were trained to see that integrity and honor were held, at least, in equal place with energy and quick-sightedness, we might, in another generation, have a different class of men in our marts of trade and exchange.

On the other hand, however, no one should fall into the mistake that his goodness and religion are everything in business. He may be very honest and very pious, but also very stupid and very incompetent. Let a wide-awake energy and keen-eyed diligence go hand in hand with religion. They will compel, by and by, a recognition. Integrity, with energy and patience, in the long-run wins.

Employers should take *an interest in the future of their young men.* I have known a young man toil late and early, with diligent care and faithfulness, to promote the interests of his employers, and after the best years of his early life were spent, to be turned off without compunction, because it suited their inclination or convenience. For an employer to do this is to act heartlessly and guiltily. When a young man has given his early life to promote the interests of his employer, it is but fair and honorable to give him a chance of advancement, and, if possible, a part in the business which he has been, in a measure, promoting. Instances of this have come under my observation, and they were alike honorable to both parties. If a part in the business cannot be given, a right-minded employer will endeavor to help forward the young man to independence. I have heard stories of the opposite thing being done; of a great trader deliberately breaking down the business of his own young men; but the meanness of the transaction could be equalled only by the wealth which made it possible.

Though the subject is important and inviting in its wider reach, we may, perhaps, more appropriately consider it as it bears directly on the family life. What I shall remark will be to the ladies of the house. If I should be thought to say more to the mistress than the maid, now, I shall be pardoned, since the former make the larger part of my readers.

How much the comfort of the family depends on those who live in the kitchen! One would suppose, were he to overhear the daily conversation when friends gather, that the crying evil of the day was bad servants. Hardly two ladies meet without mutual condolence over hired help.

There are, doubtless, a multitude of bad servants. But are there no bad mistresses? There is a very intimate connection between the character of each. I do not affirm, for I do not believe it to be true, that a good mistress will always have a good servant; but I am certain that she will not always have bad ones, and will be much less likely to have such, than a bad mistress. One who is exacting, fault-finding, worrying or grinding, will not be blessed greatly in her cook or chamber-maid.

No one should expect a servant to be in her sphere what the mistress is not in hers. *Inspire respect*, therefore. No pleasant service can be given or received, if there be not mutual honor. The mistress, to be respected, must be respectable. Here a thousand things, small in themselves, but great in their aggregate, come in. The dress of the mistress of the house has, I think, a bearing on her influence. Injunctions to care and precision in the household work come with greater emphasis from one who herself is habitually neat in attire, than from one whose slovenly looks are a perpetual example for untidiness everywhere.

The manners go a great way in moral power. We should be polite, therefore, in all places and to all persons. A mistress should be polite to her servants. To be rude and coarse to them, is to show at once ill-breeding and unkindness. Politeness has reference not only to superiors and equals, but to inferiors in social position; and is required equally by the one as the other.

Nothing more quickly destroys respect and influence for good than an ungoverned temper and hasty or irascible words. When one flies in a passion, and, on a trivial or even great occasion, loses self-control, she has made pleasant relations difficult, even when the storm has passed. Let there be cultivated such habitual self-respect, such personal habits, such manners and words as become the true lady, and she cannot but call out honor, respect and affection; she will do it naturally, as the sun calls up the vapors of the sea.

Speak encouraging words to your employés. There are a great many persons who seem to have a conscientious repugnance to saying anything except to find fault over work that is done. The employed may labor to the best of their ability, and even do all excellently well, and yet be utterly unable to tell whether they have given satisfaction or not. Now, few things are more absolutely discouraging than this. I have heard young men speak of it most feelingly. I knew them to be thoroughly competent, full of energy, and to be doing their work in the best manner, and they have said to me, "He never has said a word, no matter what I did, to show that he was pleased;" and they were glad to be free from one who seemed so incapable of appreciating faithful service. We ought to be as quick to commend as to find fault. The commendation is more powerful than the condemnation. A good word—"You have done it capitally!" "I like that!" "How quickly and how well you have got through!"—under the sound, you will see the face brighten, a smile of satisfaction spreading over every feature, and your employed goes away stronger for your service and happy in heart. You have done a kind act, and one that became you. Oh, there is a power in just a few kind and cheery words! Ye who have formed the habit of fault-finding only, learn the other way of saying commendatory things; you will find them go far and do much.

Be *sympathetic and patient* with those in your employ. Remember that the girl in your family is away from her immediate friends, that she is very much alone; while you have as many congenial associates at hand as you need, she has but few. She cannot go out to seek them just when she pleases, and so is subject to the same ennui as that which depresses your spirits, though she cannot explain it as well. She is liable to sickness, and the smaller nervousnesses which make us impatient and fretful.

We should remember, too, that the future often is not very bright. Relatives are poor and must be cared for, and so family anxiety is hers as well as yours; a burden which weighs on the spirits and makes one unconsciously gloomy and ill-responsive. You must try to enter into all this.

So you will be patient when you consider that the servants in your household are subject to all the like passions with the other members of it. They have usually no better or more carefully regulated tempers; they have not been better educated nor have they had better surroundings, that you should expect more from them. Rather their training has often been under very unfavorable circumstances. You do not know how much they have had to contend against to be even what they are.

You do not sufficiently think how much they have tried to do well even where they have failed. Perhaps the fault which has excited you was, indeed, only a misfortune, one of those occurrences over which you have often exclaimed, "There, I tried to do that just right, and see how miserably I have failed after all!" You do not think how far ignorance and vicious training, and superstition, which is born of both, have formed their characters. Be patient with them, even as you often have need of patience for yourself.

Be christian with your servants. There is a responsibility here which is not always felt. Who can say, that the girl that comes into your family has not been sent there for a great purpose by God's Providence! and that purpose to be accomplished by the influence which shall emanate from you as a Christian. Here is an immortal soul to be affected, and it is put close by your side that it may be affected by you. Is it not for our shame and sorrow that they come as inmates to our families and go away from us as they came; that often no kind word is spoken to them on the most important theme,—the eternal, and not one well directed effort made to lead them heavenward? They ought to be on our hearts. If they go away unconverted, unsaved, who shall say that ever again they shall be in as favorable circumstances; who shall say what influences of evil only shall surround them in some new home? Possibly they were sent to you that you might lead them to The Lamb of God. Have this ever in mind. Have them make, if they are willing, part of the family circle of prayer; exhibit before them—that shall be a greater power—the graces of a Christian character; by loving and tender words draw them to the Cross of Jesus.

It is possible to have those who have lived with us in these relations, bound to us by ties more lasting than time. An intercourse, on the the one side, faithful, true and affectionate; on the other considerate, sympathetic and kind, may bind them so closely to us that they shall seem as members of the family, and they shall go away from us sadly, with fond memories abiding forever in their hearts. They may look back even from the scenes of another world with joy and thanksgiving that they ever made a part of our households.

CHAPTER IX.

THE ALTAR IN THE HOUSE.

Ye shall teach them your children, speaking of them when thou sittest in thine house, and when thou walkest by the way, when thou liest down and when thou risest up. And thou shalt write them upon the door-posts of thine house, and upon thy gates; that your days may be multiplied and the days of your children.—DEUT. xi. 19, 20, 21.

Then kneeling down to HEAVEN'S ETERNAL KING,
The saint, the father, and the husband prays:
Hope springs exulting on triumphant wing,
That *thus* they all shall meet in future days—
There ever bask in uncreated rays,
No more to sigh or shed the bitter tear,
Together hymning their Creator's praise,
In such society, yet still more dear;
While circling time moves round in one eternal sphere.

BURNS.

RELIGION is a matter of the heart and belongs to a man's unseen existence; it is also a matter of the outward life and belongs to his public walks. If man were simply a spiritual essence, all that relates to God and his own thoughts and feelings might be confined to that realm in which solitary and alone he lives—his own soul. But he has a corporeal being, he lives in a world of seen things, and is in immediate and perpetual contact with persons and things as substantial as himself. His religion, then, like himself and because it belongs to his whole nature, reaches out and touches all around him. It cannot, it must not be confined to the secresy of his own bosom.

Every one who takes a broad or accurate view of man, must acknowledge that there ought to be some public recognition of God by any one who professes to believe in Him. This needs to be stated only, not argued. He who never in any form makes an acknowledgement of God, who does not at times before men take the posture of devotion, or show, by some seen act, that he recognizes the fact of God's existence and his own relations to the Infinite One, can make no claim to the title of a believer.

Since religion is more than a matter of the heart, it demands an outward manifestation. How long, think you, were every form of public religious service to be withdrawn, would it be before all religion would be gone from the earth? Were every church to be not only closed but removed, so that not even crumbling walls or deserted precincts should speak of Him who was once worshipped there; were there to be no assemblings for prayer and praise, no voice heard calling on God; were religion, all over the earth, to be shut up in each man's bosom, a generation would scarcely have gone by before the very idea of God had vanished from the apprehension of men.

The instincts of man, however, make such an inward limitation of religion impossible. The heart within, confined and imprisoned, breaks forth at the door of the lips in prayer and adoration; the man in his complex personality cries out, I must show forth what is within; my soul unseen worships the Unseen God; but this eye looks out upon His works, this body lives among the visible things of His hands; there are other men who with me live and have their being in Him; before them and with them I must worship God. No command is needed; public worship of God goes hand in hand with the recognition of God.

In this way it comes to pass that all thinking persons acknowledge the importance of outward religion—of public divine worship. To a christian man it becomes a necessity. He must have his closet, a secret place, in whose retirement he may tell the story of his wants and his cares in the ear of a compassionate and sympathizing Father; but he must also have the goodly assemblings of his brethren, in whose company he may sing the songs of Zion, and with whom he may call upon the name of Zion's King. He has a God whom he acknowledges, and whose favor he seeks when alone; that God he must honor and worship in the presence of other men. He has a private religion; he has also a public religion. He cannot be satisfied to worship Jehovah only where no eye can see him; his heart craves in all humility and sincerity that, abroad and with his fellow-men, he may bring his tribute, lowly though it be, of gratitude and love. So out of the closet grows the temple. The one is as necessary as the other. The one is the place where a lone soul holds intercourse with an unseen God; the other where the man with men looks upward to the Creator, Preserver and Lord of them all.

Between these two there is a sphere of thought and of influence, more important, perhaps, than either—The Family. It stands midway between the secret and the public life of a man, and vitally affects them both. Here a man spends a large part of his life; from it he derives the chiefest good of earth; here are his highest joys; here are his profoundest sorrows; here are his hopes and fears; here the fountain whence flow streams which make pleasant or weary his way; here are his loved ones; here those in whom and for whom he lives; here those whom he is set to guard and guide, whose destiny he shapes for the eternal years.

Now we may appropriately ask:—Shall this family life, all precious in its surroundings, and all potent in its power, be without Religion? The man has a private religion, he has a public religion, shall he have no family religion? There is a shrine, unseen by mortal eye, where he bows before God; there is a temple where, with fellow-men, he offers up his incense of prayer and praise; shall there be no altar in the household at which with wife and children he may worship? He acknowledges God in secret, he acknowledges Him in public; shall he not acknowledge him in the family?

If it be answered that form or outward observance is not necessary, that it is enough when a man prays in secret and in public, I answer:—all the reasons impelling him, in either of those circumstances, should move him here. Is there, can there be, such a thing as Family Religion, a religion of the household? If there is, then there must be for its very existence an *outward form* of some kind. It is in its very nature a visible thing, precisely as is public or social religion. If God be acknowledged at all in the family, it must be by an external service; any other acknowledgment is, in the nature of the case, impossible.

We are thus brought to the question:—How shall this recognition of God, as the God of the family, be made, and what shall this outward service be? The answer at once comes up, in two words, full of hallowed significance and association—FAMILY WORSHIP. There must be a time when the family, as a family, come together, and in their organic capacity worship God. If there be no such time and no such worship, the family, as a family, is without God.

It ought not to be necessary to press this point with argument. It would seem that a very little sober and honest reflection would conduct one to the duty of family worship. Nor ought it to seem only a *duty*. Like prayer itself, it grows out of the necessities of our nature. To one who rightly feels the exigencies of his position, as the head of a family, it commends itself as a privilege which must not be forgone. What! exclaims such a father, shall the heathen have their household gods, and shall not Jehovah God be acknowledged in my family? Shall we possess all the unspeakable blessings which revolve in our family circle, coming from the hand of the Infinite Giver, and no voice of recognition here be heard? Shall we have peace, and health; shall we have smiles and joys; shall we lie down on angel-watched pillows; shall we wake with numbers unbroken; shall we have care and love, boundlessly forbearing and compassionate through Jesus Christ, and no note of thanksgiving go forth from our lips? It cannot, it must not be! No, no, while this dear bond holds us together, while we are a family, while there is a fireside, while we have a home, there shall be an altar of praise and prayer, round which we will gather and on which we will lay our offerings! It would wrong our hearts were there no such offerings, and ours would be a home desolate without the altar; its sweetest and best hour would be gone, the hour of our family prayer!

What would a family who have learned the blessedness of household worship do without it? There are common joys which make them greet each other with smiles, while their hearts overflow with gladness;—the family worship gives them united expression, as songs of praise are mingled there. Sorrows, too, enter there, great sorrows, in whose presence they stand wringing each other's hands, and leaning heavily on each other's shoulders in agony;—the family worship softens the grief as they tell it to their Father God. The family has cares and anxieties which are felt by all its members; they have hopes and plans on which a great future hangs; they talk them over in the family circle;—it would be hard could they not bring them before God! Tell us not, exclaims such a family, of the *duty* of family prayer! When our hearts have grown so wayward and ungrateful as to forget the God of the family; when the sweet name of home has lost its charm, when we have no joys, when our hearts are stricken with no sorrows, when we have no cares and no hopes, then we will think it duty only; now we will call it privilege—the family Altar our family Blessing!

What a reflex power goes forth from the altar in the house! See how it touches the father who offers the incense upon it. There is an hour when, as the priest of his house, he is to assemble the family, and with them, and for them, present the daily sacrifice of prayer and praise. He will take God's most holy Word in his hand and read from its sacred pages; he will bow with them, and, in the hearing of them all, draw near and seek to enter even into the presence-chamber of the Most High. Confession and thanks will be uttered; help will be implored and consecration will be made; the fragrant name of Jesus will be on his lips. Now, who can be insensible to the hallowed power of all this, as he looks forward to the hour which will come in its inevitable succession? Who will not be moved by it, as he remembers it just passed? Who that has ever been familiar with family worship has not felt it? You have been tempted to be harsh or irascible; hasty words have almost burst past the watch at the door of your lips; your spirit has been disturbed, and was just about to pour forth its troubled waters; but you have remembered the silent group and still hour of the family prayer, the open, perhaps the condemning Scripture, the prayer in the ear of God. Now the mild yet searching light streams backward, a low voice whispers gently, and, as you listen, you grow calm again. The priest must not go thither with angry brow and disordered robe! So the family worship has helped you before you have approached the altar.

Who shall measure the influence of Family Worship on the household? Think, for example, how *it helps the government and training of children.* Will you find another place where the great lessons of life can be given at once so delicately and so forcibly? Here is God's Word adapted to your child's or your servant's case. You can select it for its adaptation, and, if no more, can have it make its own appeal or warning or reproof, falling on the ear of all, but touching with unseen power the delinquent one. It becomes the material of the prayer which follows, and the lesson is never afterward forgotten. Many a little and bigger heart has ached, many a silent tear of repentant sorrow has fallen unnoticed by all except God, while the low voice of father or mother has confessed and asked forgiveness for family sins. A parent who has no family worship is without the most potent of all helps to family training.

Think, too, how these morning and evening assemblings lift out of the stream those rocks which disturb the placid waters of the household life. Selfishness and petulance have time to rest and think; it is hard to hold resentment, or be unkind to brother or sister who kneels at your side. This hour dissipates many a murky cloud, and through its rifts lets down sunshine on the family group.

An imperceptible, unrecognized, yet pervasive power is perpetually, like unseen magnetism, streaming out from the family altar over the life of your child. The simple coming together for the service! How shall the child, who, morning and night since its first conscious recollection, has been accustomed to kneel while a low voice was speaking to The Unseen, ever shake off the fact that there is a God with whom he has to do? That idea has been inwoven with the whole texture of his being. Each morning and evening the golden thread has been run, until the thought of God, and his relations and obligations to Him, have become a part of his very life.

The mere taking reverently up the word of God, the slow turning of its leaves, become arguments which no coming years of doubt or unbelief shall dislodge. That it is God's book (especially if he has heard, as some of us have, the opening words, "Let us read the word of God," from a father's lips) was the first thought of infancy, and it has grown clearer day by day. Now, even after years have fled, its words are associated with that familiar voice to which he listened, half dreamily in the olden time. Can he ever believe that it is not divine? Scepticism can do much; but it must work ruthlessly if it tears out that conviction. With it will come the quivering fibres of a heart which vibrates at a father's remembered voice, or a mother's form seen through the mists of years at his side.

Who can measure the power of the prayers of the family altar? I do not mean, now, prayer as measured by the divine blessing which it obtains, but that influence which a parent's words of prayer have over the heart and life of a child.

It would not be strange if you, whose earliest memories are connected with family worship, could look back to thoughts and feelings awakened at those hours, which have been living and dominant in your souls ever since. But there are a multitude more that you do not recognize as coming thence, all of which had there their birth. No man can tell what they have done for him—that ever-recurring approach to God, that reiterated familiarity with divine things in those solemn communings of the soul before God! What trains of thought have been started, what emotions have been awakened, what soul impulses have been given! The eternal future shall only make them known. Oh, how many a resolution has been fixed, how many a purpose formed, as the boy, half-seated, half-kneeling on the floor, has listened to words of pleading with God on his behalf! How often has the heart been burdened with the heavy consciousness of unforgiven sin; how often the bosom heaved with an unuttered longing to be a better child; how many a reaching forward of thought to that dread eternity beyond the grave; how many a wonder whether, by and by, heaven would be, with father and mother, the home of the soul; how many an apprehension lest the second death should be its doom! From such impressions, made at the family altar, the child has risen up with his whole being moved, and with thoughts that shall lift his soul upward forever.

Perhaps all that I have written of the value and power of family prayer may be acknowledged by my reader, and yet he has never had a family altar. It is not necessary to follow all the excuses which are given for its neglect. The *want of time*, is often pleaded. But fifteen minutes morning and night would be sufficient, perhaps, as a rule, for all that need be spent in the service. Five minutes in singing, five in reading the Bible, five in prayer, might fill the allotted time. It had better be short, and the service such that not the littlest of the household need be wearied. It is difficult to believe that these few moments could not be secured in almost any family.

That you have *never had the altar of prayer* in your home can scarcely be an excuse for not setting up its stones. A neglected duty becomes none the less a duty by further neglect. That you have lost so much already is not a reason that you should lose more hereafter.

That you *have never been accustomed to pray before others*, ought to be no reason that you should not with your wife and children. Often has a man's religious life begun in reality only when he has first bowed in prayer with them. The perplexities and doubts and fears that oppress your heart perhaps would all float away in that atmosphere of household consecration, praise and prayer.

You may *have no words now*, but there is the Lord's Prayer, that you could speak, and if your heart were in the service, the prayers would come welling of themselves from within. A will would make a way for you here.

You do not know all that your children think of the utter absence of prayer from your home. Perhaps my reader is a professing Christian. If you only knew your children's talk with one another, you would perhaps blush for very shame. There may, too, come a time when you will bitterly mourn that you did not break over every obstacle, and, with your family, worship your Father in Heaven.

"I shall never forget," says Dr. Norman McLeod, "the impression made upon me the first year of my ministry, by a mechanic whom I had visited, and on whom I had urged the paramount duty of family prayer. One day he entered my study, bursting into tears, as he said, "You remember that girl, sir: she was my only child. She died suddenly this morning. She has gone, I hope, to God. But if so, she can tell Him what now breaks my heart—that she never heard a prayer in her father's house, or from her father's lips! O, that she were with me but for one day again!"

A young husband and wife may be reading this—Let me say to you what I have said in another place—Pray together. Have a fixed hour, sit side by side while you read, kneel side by side while you pray with audible voice. No difficulties of beginning will confront you by and by, and the memory as well as the living power of these early days of worship will be sweet and blessed.

While I would not attempt to give extended rules for family worship, the following general suggestions may not be amiss. Have a *set time* for it. Select the hour which, all things considered, will be most convenient and free from interruption, and then rigidly adhere to it. Let it be as fixed as the hours for the daily meals.

Have the whole household with you, the servants if they can be induced to come, and are not detained by religious scruples; but certainly all the children. Do not permit the youngest to be absent from the room. Let the mother hold the baby in her arms; you will be surprised how soon the little one, who is still at no other time, will, if you teach him so, nestle quietly down at the hour of family worship.

Sing, if you can, at your worship. Sing often the children's sacred songs, so that they may feel that the service is theirs as well as yours.

Read the Bible in course. While you will adopt special portions for special exigencies in the family life, in the long run, a more or less systematic reading of the Bible, book by book, is best. It will bring the whole Book to the knowledge of your household. Many parents choose to have the Bible read, paragraph by paragraph, in turn by all the family. This method does not commend itself to me as the best. It will prevent the use of some important parts of scripture lying in close connection with those which are more proper for the closet than the family circle. To me it seems too much like a reading lesson. The change of readers takes attention from the thought of the text, while the possible smiles and blushes over mistakes, or the stammering of the little ones and the poorer readers do not add to the sacredness of the word. Perhaps it is best that the father of the family, as the priest of the house, should himself alone read, and by questions or remarks, seek to impress the truths. Careful reading, in which the parent, having made himself familiar with the meaning of the Scriptures, by his manner, brings it out, will secure attention. To read well, one needs first of all, to know the meaning of what he reads.

However, on a special method of conducting this service we need not insist. A wise parent will select that which, in his circumstances, seems best. Of these he should be the judge.

There is much in the *manner* in which religious exercises are conducted in the family. The worship is none the less solemn because familiar. All the surroundings should therefore be in keeping with the hour when the family comes into the presence of the Great God. Let father and mother sit side by side, let the children not be scattered in lounging attitudes round the room and at a distance, but placed near enough to each other to make a group, so that the unity of the worship shall appear as well as exist.

Parents are not as careful as they ought to be of these outward things in a child's religious education. The little one is taught to "say his prayer"—but how? Perhaps with noise of conversation or play about him, he kneels after he has clambered on his bed, and rattles over the set words while he gazes round the room, ready with the "Amen" to burst into a laugh with those that laugh around. It is not at all wonderful that he grows to consider the whole affair as very useless and unmeaning.

Give your child different thoughts. You are doing what the disciples asked the Lord to do, when they said, "Teach us to pray." You are teaching your child to pray, and to pray aright is, as Coleridge said, "The greatest achievement of the Christian's warfare on earth."* At this hour of his childish prayer, your boy comes into communion with the Most High, and you should breathe softly, while angels listen. They see a deeper meaning in the act than you can recognize. That infant petition has in it what may touch your heart, if you will think:—

"Now I lay me down to sleep,
I pray the Lord my soul to keep;
If I should die before I wake,
I pray the Lord my soul to take."

Who can keep his soul but God? What a possibility is in that little word "if;" a possibility which darts a thrill of anguish through your breast! Into what arms could his soul nestle if not Christ's, if it should go forth from that fair body to-night?

* "'Oh no, my dear sir,' said Coleridge, within two years of his death, 'it is to pray, to pray as God would have us; this is what at times makes me turn cold to my soul. Believe me, to pray with all your heart and strength—with reason and the will, to believe that God will listen to your voice through Christ, and verily do the thing He pleaseth thereupon, this is the last, the greatest achievement of the Christian's warfare on earth. Teach us to pray, O Lord!' And then he burst into a flood of tears and begged me to pray for him."

Will you not, then, hush the room and have father and children stand silently by, as with clasped hands and bowed head your child kneels reverently at your knee and solemnly lisps that prayer? Perhaps your face will rest upon his head while your full heart joins in the petition.

It would be pleasant to believe that some who have gone with me through these pages will know the blessedness of family religion as symbolized in The Family Altar. I will try to paint for you a picture of the coming time:—The years have gone swiftly and you are changed, but the Altar in the house has never fallen down during them all. How hallowed and how dear the associations that cluster round it! You set it up—it was many years ago—when with your youthful bride you entered your new home. Your locks have whitened as you have ministered at it. The evening of your life has come. You look back through the mists that gather as you gaze, and how varied and how tender the scenes which rise to your view!

Now you see the group as it was in the long ago—the fair-haired children as they sat around, the babe hushed in fond arms at your side, when your voice had no trembling in it as you read and sang and prayed. It seems but yesterday that they all were there.

As you look, the circle has narrowed, the little ones that listened have grown and gone, one by one, out from home. They will come back no more. Some of them passed away from earth in the far-back days. They are children still. They will always be children to you.

You remember the family worship that morning when your little dead lay in yonder room, and the family, pale and weary with watching and sorrow, came in hushed silence together. Perhaps you can tell even now the scripture, forever associated with the hour, which through falling tears you tried to read. You remember the prayer as, with the sobs of mother and children in your ear, your choked voice told the story of grief to the unseen but present Christ, the long pauses when sorrow would not let you speak, and still the unutterable relief you found as, all weak and stricken, you rested on God.

Other scenes come up! Perhaps you think of the time when one of the children told you with trembling words of a new-found hope in Christ. That, too, was a tearful but not a sad family worship. How good was it to come together then! There was your child with the gleam of peace and joy upon the face; and with heart too full for words, you gave thanks to God.

Marriage days have gladdened and saddened your home. You think of the time when you knelt, knowing that it was the last that son or daughter would be there, that before the next hour of worship should come, they would have gone forth forever. How you prayed that God would go with them! You have thought and prayed for them there ever since, as though they were still a part of the circle. They are far away, across the continent, over the seas, but very near your heart and in your family prayer. So the years have gone, and yet amid all the changes, the spot where the altar stands has been the tenderest, the brightest, the dearest place in your home.

With these scenes, perhaps, come up memories of an older time, when you were young. The gatherings of your own childhood will come back no more. The family has been passing one by one away for many years. The father and the mother, at whose side you sat, and on whose knee you rested your curly head, thinking and dreaming your child dreams as the word was read, have gone, long, long ago; the brothers and the sisters who sat around, they, too, are changed, and many of them gone; they have been going ever since. Of late you have begun to look forward to another family gathering and a better family worship. It will come one day.

www.ingramcontent.com/pod-product-compliance
Lightning Source LLC
LaVergne TN
LVHW050513100826
845148LV00002B/321

* 9 7 8 1 4 2 5 5 2 1 5 2 3 *